W9-BBV-981

PEOPLE
IN THE NEWS

George
W. Bush

by John F. Wukovits

Lucent Books, San Diego, CA

Library of Congress Cataloging-in-Publication Data

Wukovits, John F., 1944–
George W. Bush / by John F. Wukovits.
p.   cm. — (People in the news)
Includes bibliographical references and index.
Summary: Profiles the life of the Texas governor, including his childhood, education, involvement in the military, personal life, business and outside interests, and campaign for the 2000 Republican presidential nomination.
ISBN 1-56006-693-8 (alk. paper)
1. Bush, George W. (George Walker), 1946—Juvenile literature.
2. Governors—Texas—Biography—Juvenile literature. 3. Presidential candidates—United States—Biography—Juvenile literature.
4. Texas—Politics and government—1951—Juvenile literature.
5. Children of presidents—United States—Biography—Juvenile literature. [1. Bush,   George W. (George Walker), 1946–
2. Governors. 3. Presidential   candidates. 4. Children of presidents.]
I. Title. II. People in the news   (San Diego, Calif.)
F391.4.B87 W84   2000
976.4'063'092—dc21

00–008141

Copyright © 2000 by Lucent Books, Inc.
P.O. Box 289011
San Diego, CA 92198-9011
Printed in the U.S.A.

Table of Contents

Foreword

FAME AND CELEBRITY are alluring. People are drawn to those who walk in fame's spotlight, whether they are known for great accomplishments or for notorious deeds. The lives of the famous pique public interest and attract attention, perhaps because their experiences seem in some ways so different from, yet in other ways so similar to, our own.

Newspapers, magazines, and television regularly capitalize on this fascination with celebrity by running profiles of famous people. For example, television programs such as *Entertainment Tonight* devote all of their programming to stories about entertainment and entertainers. Magazines such as *People* fill their pages with stories of the private lives of famous people. Even newspapers, newsmagazines, and television news frequently delve into the lives of well-known personalities. Despite the number of articles and programs, few provide more than a superficial glimpse at their subjects.

Lucent's People in the News series offers young readers a deeper look into the lives of today's newsmakers, the influences that have shaped them, and the impact they have had in their fields of endeavor and on other people's lives. The subjects of the series hail from many disciplines and walks of life. They include authors, musicians, athletes, political leaders, entertainers, entrepreneurs, and others who have made a mark on modern life and who, in many cases, will continue to do so for years to come.

These biographies are more than factual chronicles. Each book emphasizes the contributions, accomplishments, or deeds that have brought fame or notoriety to the individual and shows how that person has influenced modern life. Authors portray their subjects in a realistic, unsentimental light. For example, Bill Gates—the cofounder and chief executive officer of the software giant Microsoft—has been instrumental in making personal computers the most vital tool of the modern age. Few dispute his business savvy, his perseverance, or his technical expertise, yet critics say he is ruthless in his dealings with competitors and driven more by his desire to maintain Microsoft's dominance in the computer industry than by an interest in furthering technology.

In these books, young readers will encounter inspiring stories about real people who achieved success despite enormous obstacles. Oprah Winfrey—the most powerful, most watched, and wealthiest woman on television today—spent the first six years of her life in the care of her grandparents while her unwed mother sought work and a better life elsewhere. Her adolescence was colored by promiscuity, pregnancy at age fourteen, rape, and sexual abuse.

Each author documents and supports his or her work with an array of primary and secondary source quotations taken from diaries, letters, speeches, and interviews. All quotes are footnoted to show readers exactly how and where biographers derive their information and provide guidance for further research. The quotations enliven the text by giving readers eyewitness views of the life and accomplishments of each person covered in the People in the News series.

In addition, each book in the series includes photographs, annotated bibliographies, timelines, and comprehensive indexes. For both the casual reader and the student researcher, the People in the News series offers insight into the lives of today's newsmakers—people who shape the way we live, work, and play in the modern age.

Politics Was in His Blood

GEORGE WALKER BUSH had won a hard-fought 1994 Texas gubernatorial election against a tough opponent, and now he found
himself in front of a delighted crowd of supporters as he delivered
his inaugural speech in January 1995. Behind him stood those closest and dearest to him—his wife, Laura, his twin daughters, Barbara
and Jenna, and his parents, former president George Herbert
Walker Bush and former first lady Barbara Bush.

The newly elected governor, a deeply religious individual,
opened by acknowledging that he needed the assistance of God to
ably fulfill Texans' expectations
and that he shared their desire
to make the state the best in
the Union. He then admon-
ished his audience that "For
the last thirty years, our culture
has steadily replaced personal
responsibility with collective
guilt. This must end. The new
freedom Texas seeks must be
matched with renewed per-
sonal responsibility." [1]

As Governor Bush spoke,
his father wiped away a tear
of joy and pride, for he had
watched his son emerge from
the enormous shadows cast

*In his inaugural speech, Governor
Bush stressed personal responsibility.*

by himself and other members of the extraordinary family to become a force in his own right. The former president knew how difficult was that task, for he had accomplished a similar feat thirty years earlier. His own father, Prescott Bush, had combined a lucrative investment practice with an outstanding athletic career. Another relative served as a presidential adviser, and Prescott's father-in-law cofounded one of Wall Street's most prestigious investment companies.

Casting His Own Shadow

Through the years George W. Bush gradually fashioned his own identity. In 1989 he and a group of investors purchased the Texas Rangers baseball club, a move that drew the younger Bush away from the oil business in which his father had built his fortune. By succeeding in a field other than in oil, he earned accolades for his own actions instead of for his position as a member of a noted family or the eldest son of a former president.

Following his father's presidential defeat to Bill Clinton in the 1992 election, George W. started seriously thinking about running for governor of Texas. Laura Bush was at first dubious, because she feared that her husband wanted to enter the race only because he felt an obligation to the family legacy, but after thought and consideration the two agreed that this would be the correct move for Bush to make.

Even with his father no longer actively involved in politics, George W. was frustratingly often confused for the former president. When the *Houston Chronicle* ran a story about George W. Bush, it erroneously identified a photograph of George W. as his father. A Houston radio personality began one broadcast by announcing that "Former President George Bush kicked off his gubernatorial campaign today."[2]

However, George W. knew that as governor of Texas, he could forge an identity of his own. He fought an inspired battle to win the Republican Party's primary in Texas, even though former president Ronald Reagan endorsed his opponent. He then tackled popular incumbent governor, Ann Richards, a free-wheeling spirit with a talent for oratory that delighted her supporters and vexed her opponents. Many Hollywood luminaries, such as movie producer and director Steven Spielberg, comedian Robin Williams, and singers Kris Kristofferson and Willie Nelson, contributed heavily to her campaigns, and the state's voters warmed to the fact that Richards had risen from childhood poverty to become a success. As a result, very few political observers gave George W. Bush much chance of unseating Richards.

As the election drew nearer, support for Bush increased. He targeted rural and suburban communities that many politicians had previously ignored, and he showed surprising strength among the state's women voters. Shortly before the election, the two largest newspapers in Texas, the *Houston Chronicle* and the *Dallas Morning News,* endorsed George W. Bush.

Early results indicated that Bush would sweep to an easy victory. Enjoying the support of white males, women, young voters, and Hispanics, Bush defeated Richards by a margin of 54 percent to 45 percent. His 335,000-vote margin of victory, the largest in twenty years, was particularly significant against a popular Democratic governor in the home state of former Democratic president Lyndon B. Johnson. Bush, a Republican, had won in a Democratic stronghold.

Bill Clinton and the elder George Bush debate during the 1992 presidential race.

The Importance of Education

George W. Bush placed improving education at the top of his list of goals as governor. He stressed the importance of literacy in his second inauguration speech, included in his autobiography, *A Charge to Keep*.

Our children must be knowledgeable. They must be literate in the language of the twenty-first century. They must be ready to compete. They must be challenged to be the very best students they can be. And we must never leave any child behind by pushing him forward. I refuse to give up on any child, and that is why I argue so passionately against social promotion.

First things first. Every child must learn to read. We must start early; we must diagnose; we must get children the help they need. As my friend Phyllis Hunter of the Houston Independent School District says, "Reading is the new civil right."

Impressed with Bush's victory, the national Republican Party touted him as a possible presidential candidate. Whenever he attended governors' conventions, Bush received more attention than his fellow governors. National news magazines and network news programs profiled the photogenic young politician, who responded with ready quotes and clever sound bites.

The young man prepared to step to national prominence. He had succeeded on his own merits, yet he owed a debt to his family. Politics and mixing with people were in his blood, his heritage from birth.

Chapter 1

"He Was Always Such Fun"

T HOUGH THE BUSH-WALKER family rose to prominence in eastern banking and business circles, George H. W. Bush branched out to a new enterprise. He followed in the family footsteps in 1948 by graduating from Yale, but instead of remaining in the East he uprooted his family and headed to Texas.

The Bush-Walker Legacy

Samuel P. Bush, the governor's great-grandfather, was the first in a long family line of businessmen and politicians. After accumulating a fortune in the railroad and steel industries, in the 1920s Bush became the director of the Federal Reserve system, which oversees the banking industry, and served as a top adviser to President Herbert Hoover, who held office from 1929 to 1933.

Samuel's son, Prescott, straddled the athletic and business worlds. A superb golfer who participated in the U.S. Seniors Open, Prescott married Dorothy Walker, whose father cofounded one of Wall Street's most powerful investment firms, Brown Brothers Harriman. The Walker family gave its name to a prestigious golf trophy, the Walker Cup, and helped manage Madison Square Garden in New York, the Belmont Race Track, and much later the New York Mets baseball club.

The family's prosperity allowed it to construct elaborate retreats. Besides a seaside mansion in Kennebunkport, Maine, the Bush-Walker clan inhabited a huge estate on Long Island in New York and a ten thousand-acre plantation in South Carolina.

10

Every year the Walkers rented a train and brought in family and friends to the southern plantation for the Thanksgiving and Christmas holidays.

Prescott Bush originated the Bush political tradition. Realizing that he had earned enough money to support his family handsomely, he believed that he owed his nation a debt that he could repay through public service. This principle was translated into a successful campaign for the Senate and continuing work on behalf of charitable organizations. It was a principle that he handed down to his son, George Herbert Walker Bush, Governor Bush's father. A dual legacy of success in business and service in politics was born.

George Herbert Walker Bush made an immense contribution to the family legacy of public service. The forty-first president of the United States also had served as a member of Congress, as the director of the Central Intelligence Agency, and as a two-term vice president under Ronald Reagan. Even by extension, the Bush family had sound political connections. George Herbert Walker Bush was a thirteenth cousin of Queen Elizabeth II of England, and Barbara Pierce Bush was the daughter of an influential publisher and a descendent of the nation's fourteenth president, Franklin Pierce.

Texas Oil and Sandstorms

On July 6, 1946, one year after George Herbert Walker Bush married Barbara Pierce, their first son, George Walker Bush, was born in New Haven, Connecticut. Though the parents called him Little George or Georgie to emphasize the fact that he was not George Jr., the boy would frequently be misidentified as Junior throughout his life.

In 1948 George Herbert Walker Bush accepted a job as a drilling equipment clerk with the International Derrick and Equipment Company in Odessa, Texas. Odessa and the affluent Connecticut neighborhoods of the elder Bush's youth were as different as night and day. The working-class town sported numerous warehouses, and bars that catered to laborers dotted many streets. Simple cement-block homes housed the residents,

George W., the Baseball Player

Father and son enjoy a mutual love of baseball. Besides playing catch with his son and coaching one of his teams, George H. W. Bush loved boasting about his son's abilities to friends and neighbors. In a collection of letters and diary entries called *All the Best,* George Bush, the former president includes the following statement from an April 7, 1955, letter to a business associate:

> Georgie aggravates the hell out of me at times (I am sure I do the same to him), but then at times I am so proud of him I could die. He is out for Little league [sic]—so eager. He tries so very hard. It makes me think back to all the times I tried out, etc. He has good fast hands and even seems to be able to hit a little. I get as much kick out of watching him trying out as I do out of all our varied business efforts.

who battled tornadoes, sandstorms, heat, and drought in their quest to strike it rich in the oil industry.

Anyone who wanted better accommodations moved to nearby Midland, where hotels and more luxurious homes provided an improved standard of living. The common saying in those parts of Texas was "You raise hell in Odessa, you raise your family in Midland."

Barbara Bush told relatives that sun-parched Odessa was unlike anything she had experienced back east, where she could happily cultivate flowers and plants. Accustomed to large numbers of people and congested neighborhoods, Barbara Bush now lived in a small community situated in the wide-open plains of west Texas. Her mother, thinking that Odessa was so isolated from civilization that it lacked stores, mailed cold cream, soaps, and other items.

The first residence in which the Bushes lived underscored the differences from their Connecticut upbringing. Their rented apartment featured one bathroom, which the family shared with the adjoining apartment. To use the facilities, they had to lock the bathroom doors, then unlock them as they left. Unfortunately their neighbors—a pair of prostitutes—kept strange hours and entertained a steady flow of noisy customers. Often the customers inadvertently locked the Bushes out of their own bathroom.

In 1949 George Bush was briefly transferred to California, where he worked as a drill-bit salesman. The family lived in various motels throughout the state, and before they returned to Texas the next year they welcomed a second child, daughter Robin.

Back to Texas

Once back in Texas, the Bushes purchased a house in Midland. George W. Bush considers the town, whose population had grown from fewer than ten thousand in 1940 to more than thirty thousand only eight years later, his home, for he spent his grade school years there and established lifelong friendships with class-mates. One neighbor, Charlie Younger, explains that it was sim-ple to feel at home in Midland because of the small-town values and closeness of residents: "It was an idyllic place to grow up, a real Ozzie-and-Harriet [1950s television program about a whole-some family] sort of town, and there's a great sense of nostalgia among our group of friends for that time."[3] George W. felt such

The Bush family poses for a picture in Midland, Texas. Left to right: Barbara Bush, George W. Bush, George Bush, Dorothy Walker Bush, and Prescott Bush.

kinship with Midland that he once stated he would like to be buried there.

The family moved into a compact wooden bungalow at 405 East Maple Street, a section of town called Easter Egg Row because the exterior of each home was garishly painted pink, green, orange, red, or blue. In a vain effort to keep the constant swirl of dust out of their houses, residents constructed cinder-block walls around their cozy residences.

The walls barely made an impact on nature. George W. later recalled:

> You could look out the back window but not see the fence because the sand was blowing so thick and hard. People had storm windows on their houses not because it rained, but to keep the sand out. At school, where they kept the windows open in the spring and fall, you had to brush a fine coating of sand off the desks every morning.[4]

Though the desert sand and heat made life uncomfortable, Midland offered plenty of opportunity for those willing to risk time and money. A booming economy fueled an increased demand for oil, and the elder George Bush and other entrepreneurs hustled from location to location, seeking mineral rights and sealing deals on the basis of a quick handshake. Along with a neighbor, John Overbey, George H. W. Bush formed the Bush-Overbey Oil Development Company in 1950. Their strategy was to purchase the mineral rights on land adjacent to parcels where other men intended to drill wells. If those businessmen hit oil, the value of Bush's land would skyrocket.

Within a few years George Bush had become the accepted leader of the easterners living in the area. They valued his opinion and judgment, especially when another of his businesses, the Zapata Petroleum Corporation, successfully drilled for oil seventy-one times in one year.

Along with respect, the Bush family gained profitability. Bush's business acumen made him the area's first millionaire and enabled him to twice move his family into more luxurious quarters. In 1955 he purchased a three thousand-square-foot custom-built brick home, complete with swimming pool.

While his father built his businesses and his mother tended to the growing family—now including sons John Ellis ("Jeb"), Neil, and Marvin and daughter Dorothy—George W. roamed the neighborhood with schoolmates, played endless hours of baseball, and attended Friday night high school football games with his family. Each Saturday he met his buddies for an energetic game of football, then headed to the Ritz Theater to watch cowboy movies and science fiction shorts. Sunday religious service at the First Presbyterian Church, where his parents taught Sunday school, set the tone for a relaxed day with family.

Relationship with Parents

The Bush family is close, frequently turning to one another for advice and support. From the earliest years of George W.'s life, the influence of his parents has been constant. Like most children, George W. picked up character traits from both parents.

Most observers state that while George W. inherited his father's looks and business sense, his personality, especially his sense of humor and outspoken bluntness, comes from Barbara Bush. While her husband scoured the oil fields near Midland or flew to out-of-town meetings, Barbara took over as disciplinarian, ensured that the children completed their homework, and drove them to school and community activities. If Barbara told her children to do something, they either followed her advice or faced a stern lecture.

One time Barbara Bush accompanied her son and his friend to the country club for a round of golf. On the first hole, George W. swore out loud after hitting an errant shot. His mother warned him not to make the same mistake again, and when he again unleashed a torrent of cuss words on the second hole, Barbara ordered him off the course. George W. sat in a stuffy car while his mother and friend played the remaining sixteen holes.

In ways, Barbara Bush served as a mother figure to all of her son's friends. A succession of jigsaw puzzles dominated one table in the living room, and whenever her son and his friends entered the home, she inevitably asked them to help. As one friend explains, "Before you knew it, you were working on the puzzle, then talking about the puzzle and then telling her all your problems."[5]

Most observers say that George W. Bush inherited his humor and bluntness from his mother.

A common love of sports, particularly baseball, cemented the bond between George W. and his father. The father coached his son's Little League baseball team, and George W. and his friends watched in fascination as George Bush would trot to the outfield, place his glove behind his back, slightly bend over, and catch fly balls. His young charges tried for hours to duplicate the feat, but none could pull it off. One of George W.'s proudest days was when his father told him that because he now could play the game well, the elder George would no longer ease off on his throws.

The other children in the family and his neighborhood buddies looked up to George W., who tried to infuse a sense of fun into every activity. His sister Dorothy says, "We all idolized him. He was always such fun and wild, you always wanted to be with him because he was always daring. . . . He was on the edge."[6]

An uncle, William "Bucky" Bush, noticed that whenever the gang of relatives gathered, George W. naturally took a leading role among the younger crowd. William Bush thought that

George W.'s brothers and sister deferred to his judgment and looked to him for guidance.

Even at a young age George W. possessed many mannerisms normally found in adults. At the Sunday barbecues hosted for family and friends or at one of the many cocktail parties thrown by his father, George W. had a friendly word for each person. He felt comfortable in crowds, whether his own age or much older.

The Loss of a Sister

George W. was especially close to his younger sister, Robin. Only three years older than she, he felt a sense of obligation that older brothers often assume for younger sisters.

One February morning in 1953, only two weeks after the birth of the Bushes' third child, John Ellis "Jeb" Bush, four-year-old Robin awoke and told her mother she felt too tired to go outside and play. Barbara Bush contacted the family physician, Dr. Dorothy Wyvell, who ordered a series of tests for the youngster. The results indicated that Robin had leukemia, a deadly form of cancer. As Barbara Bush recalls, Dr. Wyvell informed the parents that no cure yet existed for the form of leukemia Robin had, and advised the parents "to tell no one, go home, forget that Robin was sick, make her as comfortable as we could, love her— and let her gently slip away." [7]

The parents felt they had to do more, so they contacted a relative, Dr. John Bush, a noted surgeon at New York's famed Memorial Sloan-Kettering cancer hospital. Tests at that institution confirmed Dr. Wyvell's diagnosis.

The Bushes frequently remained in New York, although they periodically returned to Texas. To watch over 7-year-old George W. and the infant Jeb, they sent from New York one of the Bush-Walker family nurses, Marion Fraser. Robin would also be in Texas for short stints between tests and treatment.

The Bushes had little choice but to prepare for Robin's death. They decided not to inform their son because they feared that he might unintentionally tell Robin how sick she was, and because they did not want to burden the boy with such traumatic news.

Robin died on October 11, 1953, in New York. After a small memorial service, George and Barbara Bush returned to Texas to break the news to their elder son. The boy cried and asked why they had not informed him earlier, but his parents had no words to soften the pain.

Robin's death deeply affected George W. At first he asked many questions about Robin—where she had gone, if she had been buried in a prone position or standing up, and whether she sometimes rested on her head because of the earth's rotation. At times he seemed to try and lighten the load for others. Though other family members purposely avoided reference to Robin, George W. rarely shied from talking about her. One time at a football game, George W. mentioned he wished he were Robin. When astonished family members asked why, he replied, "I bet she can see the game better from up there than we can here."[8]

One of George W.'s cousins, Elsie Walker, thought that George W. hated to see his parents in anguish. As the oldest child, he felt an obligation to make things better for everyone, and so instead of mourning he looked for ways to brighten the days.

He developed a tighter bond with his mother, whom he tried to cheer up with humorous remarks and funny stories. The two spent much time together, each quietly helping the other through their grief. One incident opened Barbara Bush's eyes to the fact that her son was doing more for her than she for him:

> One lovely, breezy day I was in our bedroom when I heard Georgie talking to a neighbor child who wanted him to come over and play. Georgie said he wanted to, but he couldn't leave his mother. She needed him. That started my cure. I realized I was too much of a burden for a little seven-year-old boy to carry.[9]

School Days

George W. did well at Sam Houston Elementary School and San Jacinto Junior High, both academically and socially. He maintained decent grades, although he could also squeeze in enough mischief to spice up the day.

Barbara Bush playfully pats her son on the cheek during a family celebration in Kennebunkport, Maine.

In his fourth-grade music class, he painted sideburns on his face to imitate Elvis Presley. While the stunt amused his classmates, the music teacher saw little humor in the situation and dispatched Bush to the principal's office. When he strutted into the office with a cocky attitude that he had done nothing wrong, the principal paddled him with a board.

Generally, his elementary and junior high school years were idyllic. In seventh grade he starred as the football team's quarterback and served as class president. He played baseball for hours and memorized the starting lineups of each major league baseball team. He and his buddies rode bicycles and traversed nearby fields in search of adventure. One friend, Bill Sallee, recalls:

> We'd crawl underneath the stadium and get up on the crossbars. We used to swing up there like a couple of monkeys. If anybody had ever slipped, they'd have killed themselves. Hell, you were a story and a half up. There were light poles that go around the stadium. We climbed all over those things, too.[10]

George Bush plays with the family dog while George W. (far right) and the rest of the family look on.

In 1959 the family relocated. The oil boom had slowed in the Midland area, so the elder Bush decided to experiment in offshore drilling in the Gulf of Mexico. To be closer to the Gulf, he moved his family to Houston and placed George W. in the exclusive Kinkaid School for eighth and ninth grades, where the effervescent youth again excelled in sports and making friends.

However, the son's true education had not yet begun. Thus far George W. had attended a local school, then returned home each night for fun, dinner, and homework. He could count on family and longtime friends for help with problems.

That situation changed in 1961, when his parents enrolled him in one of the nation's most highly regarded preparatory schools, Phillips Academy in Andover, Massachusetts. He now had to rely on his own talents to navigate rocky times. At Phillips Academy, and then at Yale University, the adult George W. started to emerge.

Chapter 2

"He Liked Being Liked"

GEORGE W. BUSH arrived in Andover in September 1961. The school has an illustrious history, for it has been attended by noted figures since its inception during the American Revolution in 1778. Bush's own father had been a student there, and now he was to begin a similar experience.

A Strange New World

The oldest incorporated boarding school in the nation— American Revolutionary patriot Paul Revere designed the school's engraved seal—Phillips Academy stands twenty miles north of Boston in the Massachusetts countryside. Supreme Court Justice Oliver Wendell Holmes; child expert Dr. Benjamin Spock; the inventor of the telegraph, Samuel Morse; and, for a short time, actor Humphrey Bogart had been Phillips students.

Bush lived in a dormitory called America House, a venerable building in which Samuel Francis Smith had written the patriotic tune "America" in 1832. The school's structured program starkly contrasted with the freedoms to which most new enrollees had been accustomed. Each morning after breakfast the boys, bedecked in coats and ties, attended compulsory chapel service. They then shuffled to classes until early afternoon, engaged in vigorous sports activities for two hours, then returned to the classrooms until 6 P.M. Demerits were meted out to any boy who arrived late for class, and after a certain number of demerits the student received a punishment, such as being confined to his dormitory. *Time* magazine placed the school on the

Bush at Andover

George W. Bush loved to poke fun at the rules that restricted students at Phillips Academy. A friend of Bush, Mike Wood, recalled what his classmate was like for the *Chicago Tribune*. The school's dress code required each student to wear a coat and tie in the dining hall, but Bush usually donned a T-shirt.

"I remember particularly one he had," said Wood. "It showed a line, creating a small hill, just a bump. And underneath that it said, 'Ski Midland.' George would wear his 'Ski Midland' shirt and some ugly tie and whatever Army fatigue jacket he could get away with."

cover of its October 25, 1962, issue and rated Phillips the toughest preparatory school in the nation.

Many new students passed through a shaky adjustment. George W. realized he was in trouble with his first English assignment, in which he had to write about an emotionally powerful moment. Trying to impress the instructor, George W. leafed through his thesaurus seeking a synonym for "tears," and settled on the word "lacerates." When the paper was returned, Bush stared at bold red letters proclaiming the paper "Disgraceful" and a message asking him to "See me immediately."

George W. wondered how he would ever avoid flunking out of Phillips. One of his friends at the school, fellow Texan Clay Johnson, said "We were in way over our heads in a foreign land. We found we had to struggle just to catch up with everybody else."[11]

Though he had trouble in mathematics as well, Bush earned average grades that first year. He also made enough friends to ensure that he did not miss being at home. During the first few months, Barbara Bush walked down the driveway each day to meet the mailman in hopes of receiving a letter from her son, but usually walked back to the house empty-handed. "I was homesick, but the child obviously wasn't,"[12] she later explained.

Though he was an average student and athlete, George W. rarely had difficulty fitting in with new people. He left an impression when it came to socializing, where he occupied center spot in the so-called popular crowd.

Most of his classmates looked up to him as a leader with an engaging personality and dubbed him "Lip" because he had an opinion on everything and involved himself in so many activities. He played in a rock-and-roll band called the Torqueys and was the school's head cheerleader for sports. He was even pictured in the yearbook organizing the annual stuffing of the cheerleaders into a phone booth.

Because he believed that too many students lacked diversion from their schoolwork, he organized the school's stickball league. The sport had been popular before he arrived, but Bush brought a new level of structure to the activity by encouraging every student to participate and by giving unusual names—the Crotch Rots, for example—to the teams. When an untalented student once caught a difficult fly ball, Bush halted the game and led everyone in a rousing chorus of cheers and applause to make the ungainly boy feel he was an important part of the proceedings.

Phillips Academy head cheerleader, George W. Bush, poses for a yearbook picture with his squad.

Bush reveled at the center of constant activity. Bob Marshall, one of his friends, states, "He sort of liked to be a little bit of a showman. He liked being liked, or getting people to like him, and it was one of those things where everybody in the whole school would know who you are." [13]

Bush later claimed that his years at Phillips proved valuable. Challenged by so many top-caliber individuals, he maintained, he learned the importance of setting high goals. He also realized that no matter where he was, he could readily make new friends and succeed in his endeavors.

Life with Father

At Phillips Academy, Bush encountered a phenomenon he would face all his life—comparisons with his father. George H. W. Bush had left a formidable imprint at the school, where he had won twenty-three different honors, including Best All-Around Fellow, president of his senior class, and captain of the baseball team. No matter what George W. did, he was always judged according to his father's accomplishments.

The comparisons did not seem to bother young George. Another student, Peter Neumann, mentioned that George W.

> idolized his father. I think he wanted to do everything he could to be just like his dad. He wanted to play baseball just like his dad did. He wanted to go to Yale, just like his dad did. And he was the first son, that was important, and so he was going to be just like his dad. [14]

During summers, his father arranged various jobs so George W. could earn some money and gain valuable experience. The younger Bush worked at a prestigious Houston law firm in 1962, as an Arizona ranch hand in 1963, and as a campaign aide for his father's Senate race in 1964.

Though fellow students knew his father by reputation, few thought that George W. would follow him into politics or match his business successes. George W. rarely engaged in serious discussions or displayed an overriding passion in life. The only indication that politics intrigued him occurred in his senior year, when he returned from home with a book written by a current United

A Valuable Education

George W. Bush enjoyed his days at Phillips Academy. He formed life-long friendships and gained a sense of discipline that many teenagers do not develop until later in life. He also discovered a love for a subject he had previously ignored, mainly through the efforts of an influential teacher, as he explains in his autobiography, *A Charge to Keep:*

> [Phillips Academy] taught me how to think. I learned to read and write in a way I never had before. And I discovered a new interest, one that has stayed with me throughout my adult life. It was sparked by a great teacher, Tom Lyons, who taught history. He had a passion for the subject, and an ability to communicate his love and interest to his students. He taught me that history brings the past and its lessons to life, and those lessons can often help predict the future.

States senator. His class president, Dan Cooper, says, "I would never have guessed he would go into public service. He never showed the slightest inclination toward it. I would have bet money that he would have turned out to be an investment banker living in Greenwich and happily belonging to the country club." [15]

To Yale

When George W. told a dean at Phillips of his desire to attend Yale, the dean urged him to look elsewhere, advising him that his grades and achievements would not gain him admission to such a prestigious university.

Bush applied to Yale nevertheless, but to be safe he also applied to the University of Texas. He told a few friends that he would not mind going to Texas, but no one really believed him; they assumed he was rationalizing his possible rejection by Yale However, all thoughts of another university ended when he received his Yale acceptance letter.

In September 1964, along with former Phillips Academy classmates Clay Johnson and Robert Dieter, Bush entered Yale University. The incoming freshman class included Olympic swimmer Don Schollander, who garnered four gold medals in the 1964 Olympics, and Oliver Stone, who would later direct such outstanding films as *Platoon* and *Wall Street.*

The easygoing Bush quickly made new friends. One, Roland Betts, claims that while other freshmen were haplessly trying to orient themselves in a different setting, Bush seemed to know every freshman in the all-male class by name within three months. When a classmate learned that his mother had died, Bush went from door to door getting signatures on a sympathy card.

"He could capture somebody's essence very quickly," says classmate Lanny Davis of Bush:

> What I remember is sitting around with George listening to his analyses of people. He was extremely witty, which is something I don't see in his public persona today. Was he a spoiled, wealthy kid? Absolutely not. The one thing he conveyed was a lack of pretense. You would never have known who his father was, what kind of family he came from.[16]

Calvin Hill, who compiled a superb National Football League career following Yale and whose son, Grant Hill, starred in the National Basketball Association, states that Bush treated everyone with respect and that it was obvious his parents had done a good job raising him.

As at Phillips Academy, Bush made a greater impact socially than academically. Few professors recall much about Bush, and one does not even remember his being in class of only fifteen students.

Bush's fellow classmates rarely considered him to be one who would go on to fame in business or politics. Robert Birge, who became one of Bush's closest Yale friends, states that "If I had to go through my class, and pick five people who were going to run for president, it would never have occurred to me he would ever run. He did not carry himself like a statesman. He had good useful opinions but there were others in the class who came across as born leaders."[17]

Bush admits he was not then a profound student. "I was never a great intellectual. I like books and pick them up and read them for the fun of it. I think all of us [he and his siblings] are basically in the same vein. We're not real serious, studious readers. We're readers for fun."[18]

The Fraternity Scene

The mid-1960s produced some of the most emotional crises in American history. The civil rights movement vied with the war in Vietnam for front-page attention, and debate over those issues was integral to campus life. Students at Yale and elsewhere argued the pros and cons of major events and demonstrated, usually for civil rights and against the war.

Though surrounded by controversy, Bush let little of it affect his life at Yale. He preferred the old-time college rituals of parties, football weekends, and fraternity events. Similar to the stereotypical image in movies of the untidy college party animal, Bush frequently walked about campus wearing dirty T-shirts he retrieved from the dorm-room floor.

To enhance his social life, in his sophomore year Bush joined the same fraternity to which his father had belonged, Delta Kappa Epsilon (DKE). Known as a party fraternity with close connections to the various varsity sports teams, DKE was the hangout for athletes and lovers of sport. During pledge ceremonies, Bush and

Many students at Yale and elsewhere demonstrated against the Vietnam War in the mid-1960s.

his roommates were asked to stand and mention the number of people they knew in the room. Bush's roommates could identify no more than five; Bush stepped up and named all fifty-four students present.

By his junior year Bush had been selected fraternity president. Weekday classes interrupted weekend parties, many organized by Bush. Fraternity brothers do not recall Bush behaving more wildly than anyone else, but they do remember he loved to enjoy himself. Years later when Bob Dieter saw the movie *Animal House*, he swore that actor John Belushi's uninhibited character, Bluto, was an imitation of George W. Bush.

Not everything associated with fraternities was fun and games. Because a growing number of students and professors considered them frivolous in an era of war and civil rights turmoil, fraternities were a frequent target of criticism from various circles. In November 1967, the campus newspaper *Yale Daily News* accused fraternities of harming their pledges during initiation ceremonies. The *New York Times* picked up the story and claimed that some pledges had even been branded with a hot iron. In defense of fraternities, the *Times* included a quote from

You're Under Arrest!

Twice during his days at Yale, Bush landed in minor trouble with the law. Neither incident earned a suspension or any action by the university, but they illustrate that for Bush, college was a time to have fun. In his autobiography, *A Charge to Keep*, George W. Bush explains the two affairs.

We charged onto the field [when the visiting Yale team upset Princeton University at Princeton, New Jersey to win the Ivy League championship] to take the goal post. Unfortunately, I was sitting on the crossbar when campus security arrived. The police were not nearly as impressed with our victory as we were. We were escorted off the field and told to leave town. I have not been back [to Princeton] since. In another not-so-proud-moment that I later described as the infamous 'Christmas wreath caper,' some friends and I decided to liberate a Christmas wreath from a local hotel to dress up the DKE house for an upcoming party. We were apprehended for disorderly conduct; we apologized and the charges were dropped.

DKE president George W. Bush, the first time his name appeared in a newspaper. The article stated, "George Bush, a Yale senior, said the resulting wound is 'only a cigarette burn,'"[19] from which no scarring resulted.

Other fraternity members explained that the newspapers made a big issue out of nothing. Though the articles cast fraternities in a negative light, the criticism died down as the year unwound.

To His Father's Defense

At Yale as at Phillips, Bush had to deal with his father's distinguished record. In George W.'s freshman year his father ran for the U.S. Senate in a heated campaign against liberal incumbent Ralph Yarborough. Mock elections conducted in Yale dormitories handed Bush the nod, but in the general election Yarborough won by three hundred thousand votes.

Young George was deeply disappointed by his father's loss, but his reaction was even stronger later when campus protest erupted in opposition to the Vietnam War, and many Yale liberals assailed his father's staunch prowar stance. One day George W. spotted the university chaplain, William Sloane Coffin Jr., a former classmate of his father's. George W. walked over and introduced himself, and the chaplain replied, "Oh, yes. I know your father. Frankly, he was beaten by a better man."[20] Coffin does not remember the incident and doubts he would be so harsh, but Bush asserts it happened.

George W. detested what he saw as arrogance by Coffin and other protesters and his pride in his father was unshaken. The elder Bush had succeeded by outworking his rivals, and the son was not about to let anyone think less of him because of it.

In the spring of 1968 the elder Bush, now a member of the House of Representatives, voted in favor of the Fair Housing Act. This law made it illegal to refuse to sell homes to people on the basis of color, and as such was controversial in southern states and in Texas. Though many of his constituents urged Bush to vote against the law, he followed his conscience and supported the measure. A proud son praised his father for refusing to yield to public pressure.

No Protesting for Bush

Though students at colleges and universities across the country participated in antiwar marches, signed petitions, or burned draft cards, Bush was busy being an old-fashioned college student. Parties, classes, and fraternities occupied his time. He claimed it was not so much that he was ignorant of current issues, but a matter of the crowd he ran around with. In a July 27, 1999, interview with the *Washington Post,* he offered this perspective: "But maybe I just missed it [the protest movement]. I wasn't looking for it. I wasn't much of a protester. I'll be frank with you, I don't remember any of my friends protesting."

A protester burns his draft card during a demonstration against the Vietnam War.

His father stood on principle in his private life as well. In the summer of 1965 he arranged for George W. to work on an inland oil drilling barge on Lake Odessa in Louisiana. The demanding schedule had Bush working ten straight days, followed by ten days off. George W. contracted to work for a certain duration, but he quit before his term expired. When he returned to Houston, a message waited for him to see his father.

"You agreed to work a certain amount of time," said the father, "and you didn't. I just want you to know that you have disappointed me." George W. later said that those words had a piercing effect because he realized he had let down the one man he respected above all others. "When you love a person and he loves you, those are the harshest words someone can utter. I left that office realizing I had made a mistake."[21]

Because the younger Bush so highly respected his father, the continued criticism of the elder Bush by campus radicals eventually embittered George W. toward Yale. As governor of Texas, George W. refused a request for a contribution to a Yale fundraiser. He has not attended any Yale reunions and, other than the close ties he formed with friends, maintains almost no association with the university today.

The Skull and Bones Society

Returning from Christmas break during his junior year, Bush stunned friends by announcing that he had become engaged to Cathryn Wolfman from Houston, who attended Rice University. His roommates were surprised by the news because he had seldom mentioned her. However, within a few months the engagement was called off. The couple realized they had acted out of youthful innocence without thinking through the consequences.

In his senior year Bush entered the school's supersecret society Skull and Bones. Recognized as the most elite of Yale's secret societies, Skull and Bones was formed in 1832. Many prominent people had joined its ranks in their student days, including Presidents William Howard Taft and George Herbert Walker Bush. Each year fifteen seniors are asked to join, then sworn in during an elaborate ceremony in a building whose walls are bedecked with red velvet and pictures of former Bonesmen. Skulls and bones rest on tables, and each new member is supposedly required to climb into a coffin and disclose his personal sexual history.

No one divulges exactly what occurs at the swearing-in ceremony or at subsequent meetings—held each Thursday and Sunday—because every member is sworn to secrecy. The most that anyone will admit is that they discuss current topics and the campus social scene, and forge lifelong bonds.

William Howard Taft was once a member of the Skull and Bones society at Yale, an elite secret organization that Bush joined when he was a student at Yale.

George W. has come under criticism in recent years for his role in the society. Opponents claim that the organization once smuggled in the skull of Native American legend Geronimo, and that strange occurrences happen during the initiation. Members reply that the society is a harmless gathering of friends, though they agree the vow of secrecy has added to the group's mystique.

Vietnam Looms

As George W. neared the end of his four years at Yale, national events heated to a boiling point. The civil rights movement, which had battled to eliminate bigotry, lost a leader with the 1968 assassination of Martin Luther King Jr. This action, the result of hatred and prejudice, sparked a horrifying outbreak of riots in some of the nation's major cities. George W. could not understand how anyone could detest a person on the basis of their color, for his parents had always taught the children to respect all others and count each person as no less valuable than another. As a youth George W. had once repeated a racial slur, at which an angered Barbara Bush washed his mouth out with soap.

The crucial issue confronting Bush was Vietnam, where thousands of young Americans were dying. Like his father, he supported the American effort, but now he faced being sent overseas to fight a war that was increasingly unpopular among the American people. As long as Bush remained a student, he received the common student deferment from military service, but upon graduation he would lose that deferment.

He discussed the matter with his close friends. He never considered fleeing to Canada, as did some students. In fact, when one of his classmates mentioned that possibility, George W. angrily

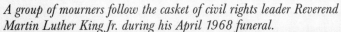

A group of mourners follow the casket of civil rights leader Reverend Martin Luther King Jr. during his April 1968 funeral.

told him it was irresponsible. Bush wondered, however, if there were a way he could enter service without being ordered to Vietnam. He believed there had to be a better alternative to being an army lieutenant in the steamy jungles of Southeast Asia.

When George W. Bush graduated on June 10, 1968, almost one-third of the 955 graduating seniors signed a petition opposing the war. George W. Bush was not one of them. He had selected his method of service—he would enlist in the Texas Air National Guard.

Chapter 3

"A Much More Intelligent Approach"

Bush took steps to solve his military predicament during Christmas vacation of his senior year. He learned that openings existed in the Texas Air National Guard, so he contacted the commander about entering. Though he did not realize it, the move would have repercussions thirty years later.

Into the Guard

In January 1968 Bush sat for the Air Force Officers Qualifications Test at Westover Air Force Base in Massachusetts. Though he scored 95 percent on the questions designed to show leadership ability, he performed poorly on pilot aptitude (25 percent) and navigator aptitude (50 percent). His overall score stood on the low end, but nevertheless qualified him for the Guard.

On May 27, 1968, two weeks before graduating from Yale, Bush was interviewed by Lieutenant Colonel Walter Staudt, commander of the 147th Fighter Group of the Texas Air National Guard located in Houston. Staudt faced many requests by young men hoping to serve with his unit—in large part to avoid being sent to Vietnam—so he asked Bush why he wanted to join. Bush answered that his father had been a pilot and that he wanted to be one also. He stated that he did not fear war duty, but preferred flight duty to the infantry. He added that serving in the 147th would also permit him to be near his Houston home.

Bush received one of the few open positions in the 147th. When the sons of two Texas senators also joined, as well as members of the National Football League Dallas Cowboys,

Lieutenant Colonel Walter Staudt, commander of the 147th Fighter Group of the Texas Air National Guard, swears in George W. Bush.

skeptics doubted that the admissions procedure had been handled fairly and charged that Bush and the others benefited from their fathers' influence or their athletic celebrity.

Though Bush maintains he would have served in Vietnam if called, the possibility was minuscule. The military draft provided infantry soldiers for the fighting, while National Guard units remained in the United States. Critics accuse Bush of purposely avoiding war duty and use his example as proof that wealthy, better-educated youth could avoid Vietnam while the poor and uneducated fought and died. When a reporter asked him in 1994 if he had joined the National Guard solely to avoid Vietnam, Bush replied, "Hell no. Do you think I'm going to admit that?" [22]

Controversy has developed about one of his answers on the Air Force Officers Qualifications Test. A question asks the enrollee if he prefers to be sent overseas, and Bush checked the box indicating "do not volunteer." In the late 1960s, overseas duty normally meant Vietnam, and critics in the 1990s charged Bush with running away from war duty. Bush says he does not recall checking the box and that "Had my unit been called up, I'd have gone to Vietnam. I was prepared to go."[23]

Bush's actions were no different than those of many other college-age youth of his day. As did many of his cohorts, he chose the National Guard as an alternative to a cruel jungle war. At the time such a choice was not seen as cowardice or as avoiding duty, but in the 1990s a different, less flattering opinion prevailed.

Bush's case was not helped by the fact that his unit contained so many sons of political personalities that it was dubbed "The Champagne Unit." Even so, Bush did nothing illegal and certainly did no more to avoid Vietnam than hundreds, if not thousands, of other young men. Supporters defend him by stating that at least he accepted military duty rather than flee to Canada to avoid service altogether. The National Guard commanders insist that he received no preference and that they were pleased

U.S. Army soldiers drag a wounded comrade through the rugged terrain of Vietnam.

that Bush was willing to devote six years of his life—two years active duty and four years in reserve duty—to the military.

Craig Stapleton, who married one of Bush's cousins, puts the issue in blunt terms. Bush, he states, "didn't dodge the military. But he didn't volunteer to go to Vietnam and get killed, either."[24]

Pilot Bush

In November 1968, after completing basic training in San Antonio, Texas, Bush left for one year of flight training at Moody Air Force Base in Valdosta, Georgia. There he was discomfited by two conditions. First, the other sixty-nine pilots belonged to the air force and knew they would be sent to Vietnam after training, while Bush would head back to Texas. Second, he observed racism in its worst form. Though momentous progress had been gained in civil rights, Valdosta maintained a firm grip on the past. Store windows still carried "No Niggers" signs, and local African Americans lived in dreadful poverty.

Again, Bush faced his father's record. During World War II his father had been the youngest commissioned officer in the navy, had flown combat missions in the Pacific, been shot down, and been plucked out of the ocean by an American submarine. However, George W. won the admiration of his fellow pilots with his quick ability to learn how to handle an aircraft.

They also stood in awe of Bush's accomplishments in the social arena, where Bush continued his fraternity ways. Whenever he went to town, Bush seemed to draw a crowd. Another flier, Joseph Chaney, recalls, "We worked hard and played hard, throwing dice and talking about flying and drinking. We went to the bar, played bar games, swapped lies. He was extremely intelligent, very witty and humorous."[25]

His fellow pilots were stunned when a government aircraft showed up at Valdosta one day to pick up Bush. President Richard Nixon had dispatched the plane so his daughter, Tricia, could have a date with the affable pilot. Bush apparently agreed to the date out of loyalty to his father, but afterward said nothing other than that the two had dinner together. Still, the other pilots were impressed by the incident.

In December 1969 Bush received his National Guard wings and reported to Ellington Air Force Base near Houston, where he flew an F-102 fighter jet. Because he excelled at what he did and because he possessed a high-profile name, the Air National Guard used Bush in one of its recruiting ads, claiming in a blurb that instead of drugs, Lieutenant Bush received his kicks from flying a jet.

Bush completed his two years of active duty in June 1970, when he graduated from Combat Crew Training School. For the next four years he served in the reserve and flew jets one weekend a month.

Between stints with the Guard, Bush worked at a succession of jobs. He rented an apartment at Houston's fancy Chateau Dijon, a complex that catered to young, single men and women. When he was not working or flying, Bush could usually be found at the pool, playing water volleyball or flirting. Don Ensenat, a Yale classmate who also lived in the apartments, says, "Dates and the opposite sex were always high on the agenda. He

Recruiting Phenomenon

During his time with the Texas Air National Guard, Bush appeared in unit publicity and recruiting material. On March 24, 1970, Houston newspapers ran the following ad featuring the young lieutenant. Bill Minutaglio includes the ad in his biography of Bush, *First Son*.

George Walker Bush is one member of the younger generation who doesn't get his kicks from pot or hashish or speed. Oh, he gets high, all right, but not from narcotics.

Bush is a second lieutenant attached to the 111th Combat Crew Training Squadron, 147th Combat Crew Training Group, Texas Air National Guard at Houston. After his solo [the first time a pilot flies an aircraft on his own], a milestone in the career of any fighter pilot, Lt. Bush couldn't find enough words to adequately express the feeling of solo flight.

"It was really neat. It was fun, and very exciting," he said. "I felt really serene up there. It's exciting to be alone in such a big aircraft and it's a real challenge to fly such a powerful airplane by yourself."

As far as kicks are concerned, Lt. Bush gets his from the roaring afterburner of the F-102.

was always enjoyable to be around." When asked by reporters twenty years later if Bush dabbled in illegal drugs, though, Ensenat denied such use. Though they had fun, he says, "We didn't do anything anybody else in their twenties didn't do."[26]

Bush had little trouble dating whomever he wanted. All the men were interested in one girl, especially—the daughter of famed fashion designer Oleg Cassini. Though every other suitor failed, George Bush succeeded in escorting Cassini a few times.

Laura Welch also lived in the Chateau Dijon. Although Bush did not meet her during this period, the quiet librarian would eventually play a major role in his life: One day she would marry him.

Business and Outside Interests

George Bush calls the 1970s his nomadic years, because he bounced from job to job with such frequency. He had not found a burning passion for an occupation, and so he tried one after another.

For a short time he helped run his father's 1970 senatorial campaign. He gained valuable political experience, even though his father lost the election to Lloyd Bentsen.

In the fall of 1970 he applied to the University of Texas law school, but his credentials were not sufficient to gain admittance. Instead, he accepted a position with Stratford of Texas, a company that specialized in agricultural development and products, owned by Robert H. Gow, a friend of his father's. Though Bush prepared well-crafted reports and presentations in his role as a management trainee, he was not fond of the experience. The best part of each month was when he had to report for weekend duty with the Texas Air National Guard.

Bush even considered running his own political campaign for the Texas legislature in 1972. He abandoned the notion after discussing it with his father—who felt that his son needed more experience before placing his name on the ballot. To provide him with that training, he directed George W. to Alabama to help coordinate the Senate race of Republican Winton M. Blount. Bush worked for Blount for six months until the November election, in which Blount's opponent won reelection.

George W. Bush gained political experience when he helped run his father's 1970 senatorial campaign against Lloyd Bentsen (pictured).

At the insistence of his father, Bush joined a Houston community organization in the early 1970s. Near the end of 1972 he visited his parents at their Washington, D.C., home. One night he took his younger brother, Marvin, out drinking, and when Bush returned he accidentally ran over the neighbor's garbage cans and created a loud disturbance. When his father asked him about it immediately afterwards, the intoxicated Bush retorted, "You want to go mano a mano right here?"[27] The elder Bush, disgusted with his son's challenge to fight and with his drunken behavior, decided to teach his son a lesson.

He contacted his friend, John L. White, who had started a Houston organization, Professionals United for Leadership (PULL), a charity that brought together professional athletes and helped inner-city youth. His father hoped that by having George W. work with disadvantaged youth he would see that not everyone enjoyed a comfortable life, that he might develop compassion for those in need, and that he might better appreciate what he had.

Bush quickly saw a difference between his world and that of the youth PULL served. One day as he played basketball with a

Favoritism?

Controversy exists as to whether George W. Bush received unfair assistance in securing a position in the Texas Air National Guard. *Chicago Tribune* reporter recounts that Ben Barnes, the speaker of the Texas House of Representatives at the time, "said he helped Bush get into the Guard by calling the unit's commander, Brig. Gen. James Rose, to recommend Bush."

According to Barnes, "I did make a call to Gen. Rose. I did it at the request of a businessman from Houston named Sid Adger."

The *Tribune* reporter continues, "Adger and Rose are dead. But John Adger, Adger's son, disputes Barnes' account, saying his father never mentioned helping the younger Bush. 'I don't know why Ben Barnes is saying those things,' Adger said."

Texas Air National Guard pilot George W. Bush poses next to his aircraft.

group of teenagers, a handgun fell out of the pocket of a twelve-year-old boy. A shocked Bush later recalled, "The kids did not seem as surprised as we were; that was life on the streets of their neighborhood." [28]

Bush blended in easily. His friendly nature and ability to communicate made him one of the most popular workers among volunteers, professional athletes, and teens. Coworkers knew he came from a prosperous family, but Bush never exploited his background. Instead, he drove to work each day in a run-down old car stuffed full with dirty clothes, old newspapers, and tattered pizza boxes. Ernie Ladd, a pro football player, claims everybody so loved Bush that they hated to see him leave.

He formed an especially close bond with one youth, a six- or seven-year-old named Jimmy Dean. Each day the boy waited for Bush to arrive, and the two would then rarely be seen out of each other's company. Bush would often purchase new shoes or pants for Dean, chat with him about sports or movies, and generally treat him as an adopted brother.

One night Bush drove Dean home. He walked up to a rotting wooden house in the middle of Houston's worst slums and knocked on a weathered door with torn screens. Through the door he could see a heavy blanket of smoke enveloping the living room, and a woman obviously high on drugs. A depressed Bush departed with a deepened awareness of the difficult lives some youth faced. A few years later Bush learned that Jimmy Dean had been killed by gunfire.

Harvard Business School

By 1973, whether due to his work with PULL or an accumulation of factors, Bush decided to get serious about his future path. Wishing to enter business, he applied to the nation's most prestigious postgraduate institution, the Harvard Business School. When Harvard accepted his application, Bush wrote a letter to the Texas Air National Guard requesting early release. The Guard complied, and in September 1973 Bush returned to Massachusetts.

Bush appeared to be the same individual as always. He walked about campus in his National Guard flight jacket and chewed tobacco, almost as if he were purposely proclaiming that he was different from the others. While classmates preferred opera and classical music, Bush listened nonstop to country music tapes. He refused to join campus political organizations or community-action clubs, partly because he hated to listen to criticism by students of the nation's political leaders, which of course included his father. Instead, he spent weekends at the Bush-Walker New England retreats and his nights at Boston nightclubs.

Those who knew Bush well, from his parents and relatives to close confidants, spotted changes coming over him. Harvard Business School pushed students to their limits. Bush had to write lengthy reports each week and attend various study groups in addition to class, an intense application to which he had not yet been accustomed. One of his uncles, Jonathan Bush, describes Harvard as "You work until midnight, one o'clock in the morning. It's just a fantastic basic training for business. It's the same thing as Parris Island [an arduous training center] for the Marines."[29]

Barbara Bush claims that Harvard Business School was a turning point in her son's life because it handed him direction and instilled discipline into one who sorely needed both. Uncle Bucky believed that for the first time his nephew realized that if he wanted to make something of himself, he had better work hard. "That kind of swagger was replaced by a much more intelligent approach to things. And I'm not sure what it was there, it may have been the peer pressure—that 'Jesus, they're a lotta smart guys in the world and if I'm gonna compete against 'em I can't bluff it.'"[30]

Bush labored hard and graduated from Harvard in 1975. He finished at an auspicious moment, for Texas was in the midst of an oil boom reminiscent of the one experienced by his father twenty years earlier. Armed with a new diploma, George W. Bush headed southwest to seek success in the business world.

Chapter 4

"To Have People Excited"

F ROM 1975 TO 1980 George W. Bush developed a purpose in life. Though he still clung to many of his old ways—especially before 1977—he emerged a more confident person who set goals and then vigorously pursued them. Along the way he met the woman who would become his wife.

Texas Oil

Still trying to decide what to do after graduate school, Bush visited his childhood friend Joe O'Neill in Midland during his final year at Harvard Business School. A quick inspection of the oil industry revealed that it offered promise to an enterprising young man willing to work hard. Bush liked what he saw and concluded that after attaining his business degree, he would return to Midland.

In the summer of 1975 Bush, now a Harvard Business School graduate, headed to Midland to begin work as a freelance landman. He earned $100 per day sifting through court records trying to determine who owned the mineral rights—the right to profit from any oil or other valuable resource that existed in the earth—to various plots of land. Once he determined ownership, he then attempted to negotiate a deal to lease those rights.

Within two years Bush had developed a reputation as a solid, if unspectacular, landman. He did not amass a fortune, but he made enough to make ends meet. In 1977 two compatriots, Fletcher Mills and Ralph Way, included him in a few deals to drill oil wells. Though he only risked a few thousand dollars, it handed him a taste of big-time oil-well drilling as well as a valuable lesson.

The first hole the trio drilled failed to strike oil—what the industry calls a dry hole—and Bush lost the money he had put into the venture. He realized that while the oil industry can deliver fortunes to those who succeed, it also is fraught with risks. He said later, "I'll never forget the feeling, kind of, 'oops, this is not quite as easy as we all thought it was going to be.'"[31]

The men drilled additional wells and finally hit oil, recovering their investment. Bush learned that the key to success in Texas oil was not to give up after a dry hole. Instead, he had to convince investors to put up more money, which would allow him to move his equipment to another location and drill again.

Outside of business hours, Bush maintained the same lifestyle he developed at Yale and Harvard. Most days he joined a group of businessmen for an afternoon jog through Midland's streets. He lived in a run-down apartment in a cinder-block garage that one friend described as a toxic waste dump. Frayed shirts and worn pants vied with discarded newspapers for space on the floors and tables. When the frame of his bed cracked, Bush tied it together with a handful of neckties. On more than one occasion Bush headed outside wearing socks of different colors, and his lack of fashion sense was so outrageous that the Midland Country Club established a prize in his honor for the worst-dressed golfer.

Laura Welch

Two factors eventually nudged Bush toward a greater sense of responsibility—politics and Laura Welch. Though he did not date heavily in his Midland days, Bush was considered one of the area's most eligible bachelors. Friends attempted to set him up with girls, and their wives mothered him by doing his laundry for him. One couple in particular, Joe and Jan O'Neill, tried to match their friend with a girl they knew.

Laura Welch was born on November 4, 1946. The shy, studious girl loved books, so it seemed natural that she should become a librarian. When the O'Neills asked if she would like to go on a date with George Bush, who had begun investigating the possibility of campaigning for Congress, she declined because

Proud Son

In 1975 George H. W. Bush was appointed director of the Central Intelligence Agency (CIA), the government organization responsible for gathering information on the country's enemies. The agency had come under bitter attack by antiwar advocates as being involved in political assassinations in foreign nations and attempts to overthrow governments.

Knowing the controversy that swirled about his new post, George H. W. Bush sent a message to his children. The following exchange of correspondence is included in his 1999 book, *All the Best, George Bush:*

> This new job will be full of turmoil and controversy and Mum and I know that it will not make things easy for you. Some of your friends simply won't understand. There is ugliness and turmoil swirling around the agency obscuring its fundamental importance to our country. I feel I must try to help. I hope you understand.

George W. Bush replied in behalf of the children. His response shows the bond of affection that united the family:

> I look forward to the opportunities to hold my head high and declare ever so proudly that yes, George Bush, super spook, is my Dad and that yes I am damn glad for my country that he is head of the agency.

CIA directors William Colby (right) and George Bush.

she had no interest in politics. However, after the O'Neills pestered her, she finally agreed to accompany Bush to an August 1977 backyard barbecue at the O'Neill home.

What happened surprised everyone. The quiet, bookish girl and the outspoken, affable Bush instantly connected, and the two stayed up until midnight chatting. The next night they played miniature golf with the O'Neills, and the following weekend he and Laura spent a great amount of time together.

"If it wasn't love at first sight," explains Bush, "it happened shortly thereafter. My wife is gorgeous, good-humored, quick to laugh, down-to-earth, and very smart. I recognized those attributes right away, in roughly that order, the night our friends Joey and Jan O'Neill conspired to introduce us at a dinner at their house." [32]

Laura reciprocated his feelings. She told her mother that Bush made her laugh and that she enjoyed spending time with him. Bush called her every day and informed his parents that Laura was "a very thoughtful, smart, interested person—one of the great listeners. And since I'm one of the big talkers, it was a great fit." [33]

George W. Bush and his wife, Laura, during his presidential campaign.

Barbara Bush perceived that this girl was different from the others when her son visited them at Kennebunkport, Maine. Instead of rollicking about the retreat, Bush rarely wandered far from the telephone so he could call Laura. He even cut his stay short when he telephoned and a male voice answered. Bush quickly flew to Texas to resume courting Welch.

Within a few weeks the two had become engaged and planned a November 1977 wedding. When Bush brought Welch to meet his family, his brother Jeb walked up, fell to one knee, and asked, "Did you pop the question to her, George, old boy?" Laura answered for him by responding, "Yes, as a matter of fact he has, and I accepted."[34] The two informed family members that they would be married on November 5, the day after Laura's birthday.

True to their word, less than three months after meeting at the O'Neill barbecue, George W. Bush and Laura Welch were married at Midland's First United Methodist Church in front of seventy family members and friends. Sticking to their preference of a small wedding instead of a splashy ceremony that would make the society pages, the couple had no bridesmaids or groomsmen.

First Political Campaign

The newlyweds postponed a honeymoon in light of the second factor that helped transform Bush into a more responsible individual—the political realm. He had hinted at the possibility of running his own campaign in the 19th Congressional District immediately after arriving in Texas from Harvard Business School, although few people at the time took him seriously. The legislator who represented Midland and the surrounding area, Democratic incumbent George Mahon, had easily defeated all opposition in his forty-four-year tenure, and most observers considered him untouchable.

Bush came to his conclusion at an appropriate moment. The Republican influence on Texas politics was slowly growing, and Mahon threw the race's outcome in doubt when he announced in July 1977 that he would not seek reelection. Bush decided to run for the position, even though he faced an uphill battle against any Democratic challenger.

His decision surprised both
Democrats and Republicans,
since Bush possessed little political experience other than working for one of his father's
campaigns or for one of his political allies. However, his childhood pals who still lived in the
area were less shocked, because
they had seen Bush take risks dating back to grade school. Various
schoolmates of Bush, from grade
school through Harvard, volun-
teered to work for their friend.

The race held the attention
of the national Republican Party,
whose leaders concluded that
their Democratic opponents
were now vulnerable in a once-

*George W. Bush talks with
Midland oil field workers during
his 1978 campaign for Congress.*

safe district. Should George W. Bush somehow produce an upset,
he would be considered a rising star in the party and a factor in
Texas politics. The 19th Congressional District consisted of immense farms, ranches, and oil fields linked by a few towns, the
three largest of which were Lubbock, Odessa, and Midland. To
sway enough voters to line up behind him, Bush would have to
convince people that he knew more than just the oil business.

He discovered that his last name both helped and hindered him.
Since his father had made a name in Texas and was currently
mounting his own campaign to garner the Republican nomination
for president in 1980, George W. could rely on his father's network
of supporters and expertise. However, he had to be careful, for if he
counted too much on his father's influence, he would fall prey to
charges of being little more than a clone of his father. Bush wished
to avoid any such comparison, so he limited the contributions of his
father's associates. He also asked his father to remain on the sidelines
rather than actively assist the campaign.

In a whirlwind campaign Bush visited sixty homes and businesses each day, bringing a conservative message of limited gov-

ernment interference in businesses and social programs and tax advantages for the oil industry. While his views received a lukewarm reception, Bush's natural charm and friendliness won over many crowds. Doug Hannah, a friend since high school, says, "He knew how to work a crowd perfectly long before he decided to go into politics. He loved it and he was having a great time. My shock was that he was such a good speaker." [35]

Depicted as an Outsider

To run against the Democratic opponent, Bush first had to defeat in the primary election two other Republican hopefuls, James Reese and Joseph Hickox. Hickox never mounted a serious campaign, but Reese hit hard and often at the young George Bush, making Bush's background a major campaign issue. At every opportunity he called George W. "Junior," even though the son does not share the same name as his father, because Reese figured that many voters would not look beyond the surface similarities. Reese also drew on a long-standing bias that some Texans hold against northeastern liberals. Bush had attended Phillips Academy, Yale, and Harvard, and Reese depicted him as an outsider who had no understanding of Texas or Texans.

Clay Johnson asked Bush how he could stand these harsh attacks. Bush had no quick response at the time. A few nights later, however, when he delivered an effective speech that drew rousing applause and wild cheers, he turned to his old Phillips Academy and Yale classmate and said, "That's how I stand it. There are some benefits—to have people excited about what you're trying to do." [36]

The Bush campaign suffered a serious blow when, one month before the May 6, 1978, primary, future president Ronald Reagan endorsed Reese and contributed money to his campaign. The Bush family angrily reacted to what they saw as a Reagan attempt to influence votes in their own backyard.

The Reese-Bush race turned into a political slugfest, with both candidates blanketing the district with posters, ads, and speeches. Bush declared his unequivocal support for the oil industry—"There's no such thing as being too closely aligned with the oil industry in West Texas,"[37] he claimed—and stated he would try to diminish the influence of government in his constituents' lives.

Reese continued to compare Bush to his father, but apparently the voters tired of the negative campaign. When the June 3 election ended, Bush had defeated Reese, 6,787 to 5,350. He then prepared to take on his opponent in the general election, Democratic state senator Kent Hance.

Bush Versus Hance

Kent Hance's strategy was similar to Reese's. He continued the attacks on Bush that Reese had begun, and peppered his speeches with accusations that George W. Bush had no political experience, that he only ran because of his father's name and influence, and that as a Yale-bred individual he was more comfortable with eastern liberals than with down-home Texans. Hance blamed all of Texas's woes on eastern-educated politicians who failed to grasp the state's uniqueness or address its problems. He stated that Bush knew nothing about agriculture and the needs of that crucial Texas industry.

Bush did not help his cause by accepting contributions from people who lived outside the state. Former president Gerald Ford, baseball commissioner Bowie Kuhn, and film producer Jerry Weintraub sent money to the campaign, as did a large number of business leaders around the nation. Hance wasted no opportunity to point this out to voters.

Hance effectively conveyed the message that he was Texas-bred and that he came from simple people. He pointed out that his father and grandfather labored as small farmers instead of amassing fortunes in the oil business, as Bush's father had done. He emphasized that Bush had yet to make a name or career for himself while he had done both, without assistance from others.

Hance's tactics found a receptive audience. Voters ignored the fact that Bush had been reared in Odessa and Midland and considered himself a Texan rather than an easterner. Instead, they focused on his years at eastern academic institutions. The attacks may not have been fair or accurate, but they were certainly effective. One of Hance's political advisers, Otis Green,

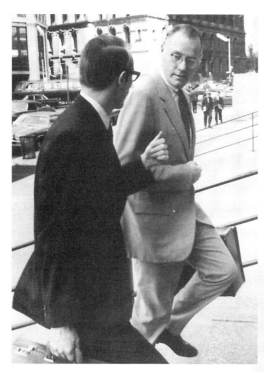

Baseball commissioner Bowie Kuhn (right), one of the businessmen who contributed money to Bush's congressional campaign.

comments, "He [Bush] had a wonderful education, and we used that against him. This is a funny business, isn't it?"[38]

Bush erred in running a series of commercials showing him jogging through Texas streets. The intention was to depict an active, youthful individual who could vigorously deal with the state's issues, but the commercials backfired. Jogging did not fit in with the cowboy image so loved in the state, and Hance quickly countered with his own commercials, in which he was shown talking with residents of rural communities and with cowboys.

Bush tried to nullify Hance's message by shifting the focus from his name to the issues. He wanted to discuss the role of government in business, the plight of the state's farmers, and his West Texas origins, but the voters were unreceptive. While Bush refused to apologize for his eastern education, he also found it difficult to counter Hance's charges.

Bush held out hope for a victory until an event near election day. One of Bush's supporters, a student at Texas Tech, ran an ad in the campus newspaper promoting a "Bush Bash" at which free beer would be provided. Though Bush had nothing to do with the event and had not authorized it, Hance quickly turned the event to his advantage. Five days before the election, he mailed a letter to voters in the district accusing Bush of poor judgment by offering alcohol in exchange for votes. Addressed to "Dear Fellow Christians," the letter stated that "Mr. Bush has used some of his vast sums of money to persuade young college students to vote for and support him by offering free alcohol to them."[39] Hance told audiences that the event might be acceptable at Harvard or Yale, but not in Texas. Supporters of the religious right, conservative Christians who advocated the return of morality into politics and carried considerable power, united behind Hance to oppose Bush.

Ironically, Hance owned land near Texas Tech on which stood a popular bar. Bush's advisers urged him to use that information to point out the hypocrisy of Hance's attack, but Bush refused. He concluded that voters would learn about the bar's existence without his pointing it out, and he reminded his staff, "Kent lives here. If I win he has to come back to live. I'm not going to ruin the guy in his home town. He's not a bad person."[40]

Bush's high-minded approach cost him desperately needed votes. In the election, Hance swept into office by a 53,917 to 47,497 margin. Bush only carried one county, but he performed well by capturing 47 percent of the vote in a district that had never elected a Republican.

He also consoled himself with the knowledge that his father had lost his initial Texas race before winning the second. This would not be his only foray into the political arena, he decided.

Arbusto

After his defeat, Bush returned to business matters. In 1977, before the congressional race, he had organized his first oil company, Arbusto, which is a Spanish word meaning "bush." With the demands of his political campaign out of the way, he could begin building his company. In March 1979 he started traveling the back roads of Texas trying to convince ranchers to sell their leases to mineral rights.

Vice President–elect George Bush celebrates his victory with his wife, Barbara, following a 1980 speech in Houston, Texas.

The outgoing Bush—aided by the attraction of his last name—proved effective at uniting ranchers with bankers, and soon Arbusto was drilling for oil. To avoid high-stakes risks that might wipe out his entire investment, Bush selected safe plots of land in the middle of areas that had already produced oil, but even with that margin his company drilled more than its share of dry wells. Competitors joked that his company's name was actually pronounced "Ar-bust-o," with the accent on the middle syllable. However, a few successes among the dry wells handed Bush a profit, and the expense of drilling the unsuccessful wells could be offset as a tax write-off.

Two years after Bush's loss to Hance, his father became vice president following Ronald Reagan's 1980 presidential election. Since he did not want to appear to be taking advantage of his father's name or to be a political liability by mounting his own campaign, Bush vowed not to run for office while his father occupied such high office. Instead, he put more effort into his business dealings. As the 1980s began, Bush stood on the brink of fantastic career success, but he faced one of the most serious crises of his personal life.

Chapter 5

"You Need to Do Something on Your Own"

George W. Bush experienced huge changes in his life during the 1980s. On November 25, 1981, Laura gave birth to twin daughters, Jenna Welch and Barbara Pierce Bush. Bush has labeled 1986 the crucial year in his development, for in that year he turned to religion, stopped drinking alcohol, and started seriously contemplating a life in politics.

Frantic Moves in the Oil Business

Now that his father was firmly ensconced in Washington, D.C., George W. turned more attention to his oil business. He called on associates and potential new clients to interest them in drilling for oil; as before, he met with partial success, neither failing nor setting the oil industry on fire with his deals. However, he impressed his coworkers at Arbusto with his ability to coordinate affairs and set goals while not impeding others' initiative.

James McAninch, in charge of production at Arbusto, recalls:

> George was a good operator—very honest and straightforward. He hired you for what you were qualified to do. He didn't interfere. He turned you loose. He'd say, "Man, it's your responsibility. You do your job, no problem." He could make quick decisions, too. He had enough savvy to ask almost all the right questions. And

[months later] he'd remember what the answers were. He was very savvy about oil fields.[41]

By the middle of the decade Arbusto had drilled ninety-nine wells and hit either natural gas or oil about half the time, slightly below the industry average. Though Bush had hoped to do better for his investors, he believed the company was on the right track and that everyone would enjoy a handsome return on their money.

Because a large number of dry wells had been dug under the Arbusto name, to offset possible negative public perception in 1982 Bush changed the company's name to Bush Exploration and offered shares to the public. He intended to raise $6 million from new investors, which he planned to immediately sink into new drilling operations. However, with the oil industry suffering declining profits, he only raised a little over $1 million.

Men work on an oil rig.

On February 29, 1984, two Cincinnati investors offered Bush a lucrative deal. Executives of a company called Spectrum 7, the men believed they could make a tidy profit by purchasing a company bearing the Bush name and led by a man who knew his way around Texas oil fields. In return for control of Bush Exploration, the men named Bush as chairman, paid him $75,000 a year as a consultant fee, and gave him 1.1 million shares of stock.

The merger enabled Bush to remain in the oil business for another two years. His good fortune lasted until the winter of 1985–1986, when a new oil crisis hit the industry. Mideast nations, sitting on top of millions of barrels of oil reserves, had been able to maintain a steady price for oil by agreeing to slow the pace of production. In the mid-1980s, however, these oil-producing nations quarreled with each other and began dumping oil on the open market. The price for a barrel of oil plunged almost by half, eliminating most of the profit made by American companies.

Some firms were forced to file for bankruptcy. Bush, who had been optimistic about his company's future only two years before, now faced unpleasant news. Spectrum 7 lost almost $2 million in 1986 and had no funds with which to repay $3 million in bank loans. Bush moaned at the time that "I'm all name and no money."[42] It appeared that he might follow his less fortunate competitors into bankruptcy.

Harken Saves the Day

In February 1986 a new company entered the scene. Harken Oil and Gas, a large Dallas firm, made millions purchasing troubled oil companies and then returning them to profitability. Its management had watched Spectrum 7 with interest, especially because its chairman had one of the most recognizable names in the United States.

When Spectrum 7 faced troubled times, Harken stepped in with an attractive offer. They agreed to absorb $3 million of Spectrum 7's indebtedness, handed Bush $300,000 in Harken stock, gave him a seat on the board of directors, and paid him $120,000 as a consultant. The deal offered Bush a way out of financial trouble and provided him with sufficient financial resources to purchase a new acquisition—a major league baseball team—a few years later.

Bush's failure to make his companies profitable added to the disturbing image that he was a feeble imitation of his father who had accomplished nothing of significance. To eradicate this reputation, Bush needed a success story he could call his own.

Religion and Sobriety Enter the Picture

Before he attained that success, Bush's personal life took a new course. In the summer of 1985, during a visit to the family retreat in Kennebunkport, Bush spent time with the Reverend Billy Graham, one of the nation's most respected and influential religious leaders. Bush listened to Graham's sermon at nearby St. Ann's by the Sea Church, then engaged him in lengthy discussions of religious issues.

The whole family gathered one evening for an extended question-and-answer session, and as Bush recalls, Graham

> sat by the fire and talked. And what he said [about the Bible, love, God] sparked a change in my heart. I don't remember the exact words. It was more the power of his example. The Lord was so clearly reflected in his gentle and loving demeanor. The next day we walked and talked at Walker's Point, and I knew I was in the presence of a great man. He was like a magnet; I felt drawn to seek something different.[43]

That weekend changed Bush. He examined the path of his life and concluded that he had been aimlessly drifting through a series of occupations with no clearly defined goals. He concluded that he had ignored religion and needed to place God in his life. When he returned to Midland he joined a weekly Bible study group of over one hundred local men and started reading the Bible every day.

This reexamination of his life led to another significant change—Bush's decision to renounce alcohol. He had always enjoyed a drink or two after the day's business was concluded, and admits to drinking to excess at times. The two times he encountered the police in college—when he stood atop the goalpost at Princeton and when he "liberated" the Christmas wreath—may have been aided by alcohol, and events the

George Bush and Reverend Billy Graham after a Sunday morning service at St. Ann's Church in Kennebunkport, Maine.

evening he challenged his father to a fight had certainly been influenced by intoxication.

Though he never allowed alcohol to affect his work or his relationship with family, Bush sometimes wondered if he relied on it too much. Two events nudged Bush into deciding that he would be a better individual without drinking. In April 1986 he encountered Al Hunt, then the *Wall Street Journal's* Washington bureau chief, at a restaurant. Hunt was eating dinner with his wife and four-year-old son when an inebriated Bush walked over. Hunt had just written an article predicting that Bush's father would not win the Republican nomination for president for the 1988 election, and Bush intended to let him know what he thought.

"You [expletive] son-of-a-bitch," slurred Bush to the startled political reporter. "I saw what you wrote. We're not going to forget this."[44] Bush then returned to his own table.

Hunt could not figure out why Bush was so angry, because in the article he had not attacked his father but simply referred to his poor chances. Hunt concluded that, since Bush was obviously intoxicated, he would let the matter drop, although he was upset that his wife and son had witnessed an important figure embarrassing himself in public.

Thirteen years later Bush learned what happened and called Hunt to apologize. Bush states that he does not now recall the event, but he feared that he had hurt Hunt and his family and wanted to straighten out the situation.

The second incident occurred on July 28, 1986, at the exclusive Broadmoor Hotel in Colorado Springs, Colorado. After a night of heavy drinking, Bush awoke with a severe hangover. He suited up for his daily jog, but because of his weakened condition he had to stop halfway through the run. Bush returned to his hotel room and told Laura he would no longer drink alcohol. He feared that it might be hurting his career, and he did not want to embarrass his father, who then had serious aspirations for the presidency.

Bush did not think he was an alcoholic, but realized that drinking had created problems for him. Life would be simpler without it, and since that weekend he has never again touched alcohol. His decision surprised his parents, who did not realize that their son had been drinking heavily.

When asked by reporters if he was an alcoholic, Bush replied, "Well, I don't think I had [an addiction]. You know, it's

Son to the Defense

George W. Bush hated to hear or read any criticism of his father, but he especially despised the 1987 article that appeared in *Newsweek* magazine. In his autobiography, *A Charge to Keep,* Bush expresses his views of the affair.

"My blood pressure still goes up when I remember the cover of *Newsweek,* in October 1987. It pictured my dad, in his boat, with the caption: 'Fighting the Wimp Factor.' They were talking about George Bush, war hero, youngest pilot to earn his wings in the Navy, a pilot who had been shot down and rescued by a submarine near an island occupied by the Japanese. How could they say that about the former director of the Central Intelligence Agency, ambassador to the United Nations and China, loyal Vice President to Ronald Reagan, and wonderful dad and grandfather? I felt responsible, because I had approved the interview. I was livid, and I let a lot of people know exactly how I felt."

hard for me to say. I've had friends who were, you know, very addicted, and they required hitting bottom [to start] going to AA [Alcoholics Anonymous]. I don't think that was my case."[45]

Bush credits Laura's support and Billy Graham's inspiration with helping him quit drinking. He never attended an AA meeting, but states that with the assistance of a loving family and religion, he has been able to live a full life without alcohol. In 1999 Bush said that the decision to stop drinking was one of the turning points in his life.

Campaigning for Dad

With the oil industry in a slump and with his personal life newly focused, Bush was ready to assist in a national campaign. His father had decided to run for president in 1988, and for two years his oldest son made major contributions.

He stepped into an important role from the beginning. One of his father's advisers, political consultant Lee Atwater, had also worked for other politicians, and George W. wondered if the family could count on Atwater when the chips were down. Employing the blunt approach, Bush asked Atwater if he could be trusted. When the startled adviser wondered if he were serious, Bush replied, "I'm damn serious, pal. In our family, if you go to war, we want you completely on our side. We love George Bush, and by God, you'd better bust your ass for him."[46]

Atwater tossed the challenge back at Bush by telling him if he had misgivings, Bush should move to Washington, D.C. so he could keep watch on the other workers. If Bush doubted anyone's loyalty, including Atwater's, he could then take quick action.

Bush followed the advice, moved his family into a Washington, D.C. townhouse, and assumed the role of what the other workers labeled the "loyalty thermometer." He made sure that everyone worked for his father's benefit and coordinated communications between his father and the campaign staff.

George W. and Atwater did not develop a friendly relationship. One time Atwater allowed a reporter to interview and photograph him while the adviser stood in his underwear in the bathroom. George W. conveyed a sharp message indicating the

George Bush and his political strategist, Lee Atwater, lead a campaign rally during the 1988 presidential race.

unprofessionalism of such a move and demanding that he personally apologize to the candidate and Mrs. Bush.

Bush disliked one aspect of his job—the daily grind of answering reporters' questions and rebutting rumors. One writer, *Newsweek* magazine's political reporter Margaret Warner, incurred his ire with her October 1987 cover story on his father, titled "Fighting the Wimp Factor." In it, Warner wondered if Bush could connect with the average working American and questioned whether he had the fortitude to stand up to serious issues.

George W. believed that the article was not only harmful to his father's image, but grossly unfair. He telephoned the reporter and pointed out that she had described his father with the word "wimp" seven times in two pages. The article helped label Bush's father as weak, and he never succeeded in eradicating the image.

George W. defended his father from another serious charge in June 1988 when the press ran stories that the senior Bush had had an extramarital affair. Atwater's advice was that Bush, instead of running from the accusations, should have someone immediately respond, get the issue into the open, and let it gradually disappear. George W. called *Newsweek* magazine, which ran a story quoting him as firmly stating, "The answer to the Big A is N.O."[47] This blunt, quotable statement met with favor from the press and dispelled rumors that his father had been unfaithful.

Following his father's victory in November 1988, George W. helped fill positions in the new administration before returning to Texas. The campaign experience had been profitable for both father and son, who had worked together for the first time and gained a higher level of respect for each other.

The two years also provided George W. valuable training in running a political campaign and an inside view of Washington politics. Though he wondered if his father's election to the presidency might make it harder for him—he feared that people might expect more of the oldest son of a president—he had positioned himself for his own attempt to gain high public office.

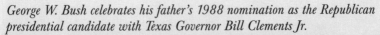

George W. Bush celebrates his father's 1988 nomination as the Republican presidential candidate with Texas Governor Bill Clements Jr.

His first step was to purchase a home in Dallas, Texas, a key economic and political center. He also asked a presidential aide to compile a report about how the lives of the sons and daughters of former presidents had been affected by their fathers' careers so he could avoid making any mistakes they may have committed.

Bush quietly let it be known that he was considering a run at the state's top post. However, people inside the state and on his father's Washington staff felt that George W. needed more exposure, that as yet he had done nothing of substance to gain the confidence of voters. Even one of his close friends and fraternity brothers, Roland Betts, cautioned him that "You need to do something on your own, need to get your own name out there and develop your own reputation."[48]

Even if he had had sufficient public confidence, Bush lacked one crucial element for a successful campaign—money. He needed enough to be able to support his family in the midst of politicking and to finance an effective political machine. In 1988 he saw a chance to gain both the public's confidence and more money.

Purchase of the Texas Rangers

Bush first considered purchasing the Texas Rangers baseball club early in 1988 when William O. DeWitt Jr., the owner of Spectrum 7, asked if Bush were interested. DeWitt knew that the current Ranger owner, Eddie Chiles, needed money, so he and Bush formed a group of investors interested in buying the sports team. Bush used his Harken stock as collateral to obtain a $500,000 loan for his share, the smallest of the group of investors.

Bush and businessman Edward Rose were selected to run the team. Since Bush possessed a well-known name and felt comfortable among people, for an annual salary of $200,000 he handled public relations for the Rangers. The quieter Rose remained in the background as chairman of the board and ran the day-to-day operations of the club.

On April 21, 1989, while Bush was still active in his father's presidential run, he and the other investors closed the deal to buy the baseball team. For the first time in his life George W. Bush had entered a realm into which his father had not previously trodden. The move would help catapult him into national prominence.

The Rangers were in dire need of help to improve a losing image created over years of poor play and bad managerial decisions. Low attendance figures continually placed the team in poor financial straits, and the team played in an outdated ball park. Roland Betts, one of the investors, was stunned when he saw the dilapidated facility and concluded that to make money, the team required a state-of-the-art stadium.

Bush worked constantly to improve the team's image in the community and carefully crafted friendly ties with the local media. He concentrated on the team's sole superstar, pitcher Nolan Ryan, as a marketing commodity to bring in more fans. To draw from the huge Mexican-American market in the area, he began broadcasting the games in Spanish as well as English.

Bush wanted to create a family atmosphere, and to that end he knew every employee of the club by name, from the star ball players to the hot dog vendors. He tried to make every person feel important to the organization and loved strolling around the

Hall of Fame pitcher Nolan Ryan.

field and stands during the game and practices, greeting each employee in turn. Fans could always count on seeing Bush in his customary seat next to the dugout for every home game, happily signing autographs and munching on peanuts and hot dogs.

He once invited his mother to attend a home game, and she was astounded at the friendly atmosphere. He seemed to know everyone there, and whenever an employee approached, Bush would introduce his mother to the "best groundskeeper in the major league" or the "finest ticket-taker in any park."

The ball players also grew fond of Bush. Bobby Valentine, a former manager, gives a typical assessment: "You know, this guy fired me. The honest truth is that I would campaign barefoot for him today."[49]

The most important contribution Bush made was convincing Texas voters to approve a bond financing a new stadium. When the new park opened in 1994, observers labeled it one of the finest ballparks in the nation. *Financial World* magazine rated the facility, which contains a museum, sports bar and restaurant, and luxury boxes, the most profitable in baseball.

Bush's time with the Rangers proved beneficial. Besides making a handsome profit from the team's popularity, Bush gained favorable publicity, not because he was the president's son but because of what he had done to make the Rangers a success. Besides, his name was now intricately linked with America's favorite pastime, baseball, an advantage when he entered the political arena.

Controversy Swirls

Two events tarnished Bush's magic touch. On June 22, 1990, Bush sold his shares of Harken stock for $4 a share so he could pay off the debt incurred in purchasing the Rangers. Six weeks later, Iraq started the Persian Gulf War by invading oil-rich Kuwait, causing shares of stock in all American oil companies, including Harken, to plunge.

Critics wondered if Bush, who gained a handsome profit in the deal, had sold his shares because he had advance knowledge of the crisis in the Mideast. He answered that he simply needed the money to pay off his obligation. Though the government

U.S. tanks maneuver through the desert during the Persian Gulf War.

investigated the incident, it discovered no evidence of wrong-doing and no indictments were issued.

The second event also involved Harken. The nation of Bahrain, situated along the Persian Gulf, offered contracts to American companies to drill offshore wells in the gulf. Most American corporations, including giant Amoco, submitted bids, but the contract was awarded to Harken. What surprised on-lookers was that Harken was small compared with its competitors, and the company had no experience in offshore drilling. Some questioned whether George W. Bush had exerted unfair influence in Washington in making the deal. Bush denied the assertion and stated that he had, in fact, advised Harken's board of directors against bidding on the contract.

Neither controversy failed to slow Bush's rise in Texas. His solid work rebuilding the baseball team compensated for a few rumors that could not be proven. He was ready for his next step—the governorship of Texas.

Chapter 6

"He's a Seller"

Gᴇᴏʀɢᴇ W. Bᴜsʜ's campaign for the Texas governor's position demonstrated that he, in conjunction with his advisers, could develop a sound plan, then stick with it in the face of adversity. Though critics accused him of capitalizing on a renowned name and questioned the propriety of his behavior during his college years, a focused Bush ignored the taunts and proposed his own agenda.

Focus on the Issues

One area in which Bush grappled with his opponent, incumbent Ann Richards, was public tax support of the educational system. Richards supported a property tax shift that would remove money from wealthier districts and hand it to poorer areas, but Bush realized that many voters would oppose such a move. He created his own plan to retain control of education dollars by local districts, which could then decide how to spend their own money.

He also supported a limit on the amount of money awarded in liability lawsuits. Texas had been labeled by national magazines as the state where individuals won more money from businesses and physicians in jury awards than any other place in the nation.

Texas Governor Anne Richards.

Bush states that "I wanted Texas to be a great place to do business, an entrepreneurial heaven, where dreamers and doers felt comfortable risking capital and creating jobs, not a haven for frivolous lawsuits."[50]

Finally, Bush hoped to reform the state's welfare system, which he believed had grown bloated and left recipients without a feeling of personal responsibility for improving their lives. He proposed that benefits be denied to children born to welfare recipients who already had two children, and he urged private charities and businesses to assume a greater role in helping those in need.

Personal Character and Temper

An issue that quickly dominated the gubernatorial campaign, and that would again torment George W. Bush in his presidential campaign, was whether he had committed any youthful transgressions. He had brought up the topic in 1994 in an attempt to show that he had grown as a person. He explained that he had matured from his days as an "irresponsible" youth, and when a reporter followed up by asking if he had used illegal drugs, Bush replied, "Maybe I did, maybe I didn't. What's the relevance?"[51]

Instead of disarming voters, the comment unleashed a torrent of questions from reporters who wondered if rumors were true that he had, for example, used cocaine and danced naked

Faith-Based Assistance

George W. Bush stressed the importance of allowing local charitable organizations to assume some of the government's burden in supporting the welfare system. He favored a program that allowed religious groups to compete for government contracts.

Bush claimed that his stance did not advocate any particular religion, but critics feared that the idea dangerously blurred the separation of church and state. Church leaders from dozens of Christian sects opposed the notion.

Charles Moore, pastor of the Grace United Methodist Church in Austin, Texas, told the *Washington Post*, "The concern that the founding fathers had about the separation of church and state was what the church might do to the state." He added that Bush's agenda "opens the door more than anything that I have seen in my lifetime to the church being able to take over the state."

at a local bar. Astounded, Bush said, "I'm amazed at how one simple statement has set off a swirl—that I'm the wildest man that ever lived."[52]

Ann Richards tried to use the controversy to her advantage. She knew that her opponent had bitterly reacted to her 1988 remark at the Democratic National Convention about the elder George Bush, that he could not understand the problems of the nation because he was "born with a silver foot in his mouth." She hoped to produce a similar inflammatory response with repeated references to George W.'s reckless youth. She also reminded voters that the younger Bush, whom she referred to as "Shrub," had risen in politics and business because of his father's influence.

George W. Bush refused to take the bait. He focused on his main campaign issues, and addressed his past by cleverly including Richards: "What I did as a kid? I don't think it's relevant, nor do I think it's relevant what Ann Richards did as a kid. I just don't think it matters. Did I behave irresponsibly as a kid at times? Sure did."[53]

Victory in Texas

Texas voters responded positively to the way that Bush refused to reply to the attacks on his past. Seeing that the momentum had begun to swing in Bush's favor, Richards increased her denunciations of his character. Rather than talking about issues, Richards made Bush the focus. She so severely castigated her opponent that even her campaign aides wondered if she were assailing him too frequently.

Richards committed a major blunder at an August rally in Texarkana when she told a crowd of teachers, "You just work like a dog, you do well, and all of a sudden you've got some jerk who's running for public office telling everybody it's all a sham."[54]

This depiction backfired with voters, who believed Richards had too harshly described her opponent. On election day, Bush surged to an early lead that he never relinquished. Richards conceded later that evening, and George W. Bush had won his first major campaign by a decided 54 percent to 45 percent margin.

The Bush Style of Governing

Like every executive, politician, or administrator, Bush developed his own routine of governing. He typically arrived at his capitol office at 8:00 A.M., held meetings until 11:30, then headed outside for his daily three-to-five-mile jog. His afternoon schedule usually consisted of more meetings and appointments, and his workday ended with an official state dinner, which he hosted for visitors or dignitaries at the governor's mansion. Bush loved chatting with his guests at dinner, but he was quite adamant about retiring no later than 9:00 P.M. so he could spend private moments with his wife and children or reading light novels and thrillers.

Because his daily calendar was so busy, Bush provided five minutes for each appointment. At the end of that time an aide knocked on his door, and if Bush indicated he needed more time the aide would automatically return five minutes later.

For longer meetings, such as with his staff or with members of his administration, Bush set aside more time, but even then he liked to keep the discussions brief. He cut short anyone who started to talk too long and asked them to come to the main issue of their presentation. During one briefing, which all presidential candidates receive from the federal government, Under Secretary of Defense Paul Wolfowitz listed the positions of the armed forces, their equipment, and other details. Bush interrupted by asking him to skip that portion and enlighten him on the role of America's defense. Wolfowitz, accustomed to long-winded presentations in Washington, said to the governor, "I wish more people would ask that kind of question when discussing details of military budgets." [55]

Staff members knew that they were to thoroughly research an issue, such as public education, before meetings, then present their opinions to Bush during the meeting. The governor liked a free discussion of views and urged everyone in attendance to take part, even if they strongly disagreed with his opinion. If assistants relied too heavily on written notes, he asked them to put away the material and mention the main point in a few sentences. After an exchange of ideas Bush decided whose advice to follow.

Bush made sure he kept open communication lines with state legislators to make the passage of his proposals more likely. Each Wednesday while the legislature was in session, Bush invited top leaders to meet with him to discuss important matters. Consequently, Bush experienced great success at pushing most of his proposals through the Texas House of Representatives and Senate, especially as a first-term governor.

Critics charged that while in office, Bush ignored many important issues in favor of his pet projects. While education and business reform received much attention, critics claimed that Bush slighted the environment, job programs for the unemployed, and minority appointments to state offices.

Education in Texas

Bush placed major importance on improving education in Texas. He believed that competent school systems benefited business in the state by developing an educated workforce, and he felt that students had to be better prepared to enter the high-tech world that awaited them.

His initial action on this issue was to try to alter the method of paying for public education. Some favored a property tax—a tax on the value of homes and businesses located in the school district. This benefited wealthier areas, which contained more expensive buildings and more extensive land holdings, and therefore could support a costlier education system. Bush, however, advocated a raise in the state sales tax. While larger businesses, which paid proportionately larger property taxes, favored this proposal, smaller concerns such as doctors, lawyers, and consultants opposed it. Because the state contained a vast segment of smaller service-oriented businesses, Bush faced significant opposition. In spite of heated lobbying by the Bush camp, his tax plan failed miserably.

Bush found greater fortune in his attempt to improve results on statewide educational testing. Scores on the 1995 Texas Assessment of Academic Skills test indicated that at least 350,000 children lacked minimum reading skills. After examining a complex volume detailing educational issues, Bush closed the report and asked his education commissioner, Michael Moss, "If you could do one thing, one thing only, to get every child the best possible start to a great education, what would it be?"[56] Moss replied he would want to improve reading skills.

As a result Bush started the Texas Reading Initiative, a program designed to develop reading proficiency in every student by the third grade. Teachers were allowed flexibility in how they improved reading scores, but a system of accountability also pressured educators to perform. Bush reorganized the Texas education code so that it included clearly defined goals and expectations.

When a group of university leaders asked Bush for $1 billion more for higher education, Bush asked if they would settle for $500 million. The educators briefly discussed the question, then answered in the affirmative. Hearing that, Bush rejected their entire request. He admonished them for being so willing to accept half of what they wanted, and told them not to return until they compiled a list of provisions that they could justify. He wanted the teachers to prove the value of any programs they created.

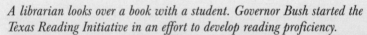

A librarian looks over a book with a student. Governor Bush started the Texas Reading Initiative in an effort to develop reading proficiency.

By 1999 Texas's new curriculum had improved the state's test results. Math scores doubled, and in 1999 Bush proudly pointed out that scores had risen in every subject and at every grade level tested each year since 1994.

This allowed him to focus on another aspect of education which he believed should be dropped—social promotion. He contended that districts that promoted failing students on the basis that it would be harmful to place them with younger groups were doing a disservice. He wanted every student in the state to master the material in one grade before moving on to the next grade.

Other Proposals

A second priority for Bush was the state's juvenile justice system. He believed that the penal structure in Texas suffered because of lax enforcement of laws and insufficient jail space. Juveniles in prison wore gang colors and had little to do, and as a result prison guards often had to break up brawls.

After passing laws permitting tougher sentences for juveniles found guilty of a crime, and after funding the construction of more prisons, Bush ordered his director of the Texas Youth Commission, Steve Robinson, to instill more discipline in prison. Juvenile offenders were required to don bright orange uniforms, rise early, exercise each day, and help take care of the prison. Everyone's head was shaved, and no inmate was permitted to speak to a guard unless spoken to. Bush contended that this military atmosphere held the youths accountable for their criminal actions and brought order to the prisons.

Under Governor Bush, the number of beds in juvenile detention facilities tripled, thereby enabling judges to issue longer, tougher sentences. According to the Bush staff, this emphasis on personal responsibility—making a youth face the consequences of his actions—has paid dividends. Juvenile crime in the state dropped 7 percent and violent crime decreased 38 percent from 1994 to 1999.

Bush campaigned on the promise that as governor he would fight to change the state's laws regarding lawsuits so that they were fairer to businesses. The system in place when he took office favored the victim against a business and allowed huge sums

Bush's Critics

While many Texas residents praised George W. Bush's tough program to reform the juvenile justice system, others condemned it as sadly out of touch with reality. Defense attorneys and liberal politicians argued that inner-city youth, particularly blacks and Hispanics, paid the price for the crackdown and pointed out that almost 75 percent of the four thousand juveniles in the state's correctional facilities were members of those minority groups.

The *Washington Post* quotes defense attorney Keith Hampton, who worked with juvenile delinquents and argues, "They've transformed a system which was founded on the notion of rehabilitation and turned it into a criminal-based, revenge kind of a system."

University of Texas law professor Robert Dawson explained that the increase in crime of the late 1980s had already begun to slow before Bush took office: "By 1995, it was already on the way down, though we didn't know it at the time. So we were reforming a lot of things after the problem had started to correct itself. Of course, that doesn't stop people from taking credit for it. But who can object to that? That's what politicians do."

in damages to be assessed against any concern found guilty of negligence or malicious behavior. Some firms had relocated to other states to avoid the multimillion-dollar judgments awarded by juries in Texas lawsuits.

Bush wanted not only to place a cap on liability judgments, but also to halt the proliferation of frivolous lawsuits filed in the hopes of winning vast amounts of money in a pretrial settlement. After negotiating with state legislators, Bush succeeded in having a limit of $750,000 placed on such lawsuits.

Bush created such a favorable business climate, and was such an effective promoter of Texas, that new businesses moved into the state. In one instance, Samsung Semiconductor investigated relocating to Texas, Georgia, or Oregon. Though all three states courted Samsung, the company selected Texas. Brenda Arnett, the former head of the Texas Department of Commerce, credited Bush with the success. "He met with Samsung's top executives. He didn't promise them anything. He talked about how much he loved Texas and why this was a good place for business, and that really impressed them. He's a seller."[57]

Governor Bush believed that the state's welfare system had grown too large. To reduce the government's role, he encouraged local communities, church organizations, and other charitable groups to institute child care programs, jobs programs, and financial assistance programs. With those steps, the government would be required to do less, the number of state employees could be reduced, and taxes could be decreased. While some residents praised Bush's welfare agenda, others criticized him as uncaring toward those in need.

Capital Cases

Bush experienced rough spots in his first term as governor, but none received more attention than the Karla Faye Tucker case and the Henry Lee Lucas case. Both involved individuals convicted of murder and sentenced to death; as governor, Bush had to make the final decision to allow the executions to occur or to block them.

The first inmate, Karla Faye Tucker, had with her boyfriend hacked to death two people in 1983. The pair were convicted and sentenced to death, but on death row Tucker became a born-again Christian. Her apparent reformation created international headlines and news articles detailed the story of an evil woman who, by finding God, had been truly transformed.

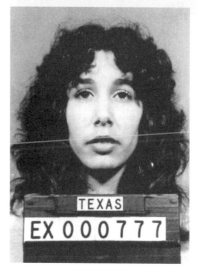

Convicted murderer Karla Faye Tucker became a born-again Christian while on death row.

Opponents of capital punishment pointed to Tucker as an example of the senselessness of execution. Since she was a different person, they argued, Tucker should be removed from death row. Religious groups, even conservative ones that normally supported capital punishment, asked for a reprieve, a representative of Pope John Paul II wrote a letter requesting leniency, and Hollywood stars urged that the Tucker execution be reconsidered. One of Bush's daughters told her father, only two days before the date of execution, that she opposed capital punishment.

Because even conservative religious groups clamored for leniency, Bush's aides advised him to grant Tucker a reprieve. They pointed out that should she be put to death, Tucker would be the first female executed in Texas since the Civil War. This would make Bush appear to be a callous leader who disregarded important facts. By granting what the public wanted, his aides said, Bush would be seen as a merciful man.

Bush followed a rigid procedure when dealing with capital punishment cases. He asked two questions—does any doubt exist that the individual committed the crime, and did the person have full access to available legal procedures, such as appeals.

Bush Replies to Tucker

After hearing the arguments in the Karla Faye Tucker case, Bush made his decision, which he called "one of the hardest things I have ever done," and read a statement to the press. He includes the statement in his autobiography, *A Charge to Keep*.

Many people have contacted my office about this execution. I respect the strong convictions which have prompted some to call for mercy and others to emphasize accountability and consequences.

Like many touched by this case, I have sought guidance through prayer. I have concluded judgments about the heart and soul of an individual on death row are best left to a higher authority. Karla Faye Tucker has acknowledged she is guilty of a horrible crime. She was convicted and sentenced by a jury of her peers. The role of the state is to enforce our laws and to make sure all individuals are treated fairly under those laws.

The state must make sure each individual sentenced to death has opportunity for access to the court and a thorough legal review. The courts, including the United States Supreme Court, have reviewed the legal issues in this case, and therefore I will not grant a thirty-day stay.

May God bless Karla Faye Tucker, and may God bless her victims and their families.

Bush insists that he will not halt Karla Faye Tucker's execution during a February 3, 1998 statement to the media.

Since the evidence clearly proved Tucker's guilt, and since her pleas had traveled through the court system for fifteen years, Bush refused to halt her execution. He believed that she had changed while in prison and had shown remorse for her crime, but concluded that was beside the point. In spite of overwhelming pressure to halt her execution, and even though Tucker appeared to have had a true religious conversion, Bush permitted the process to take its course. On February 3, 1998, Karla Faye Tucker was executed by lethal injection.

"May God bless Karla Faye Tucker, and may God bless her victims and families," Bush stated on the day of her execution. He also said that the wait in his office for news that the execution had been carried out "remain the longest twenty minutes of my tenure as Governor."[58]

The second case was equally difficult. Henry Lee Lucas had few redeeming features. At least Tucker felt sorrow for her actions, but Lucas enjoyed the publicity aroused by his crimes.

When he was convicted of the 1979 rape and murder of an unidentified woman, Lucas admitted that he had murdered many more. Bush wrote that Lucas was

> contemptible, a one-eyed drifter, a proven liar, and a killer who wore a surly scowl and at one time confessed to the police that he had committed more than six hundred murders, including that of his own mother. At the height of his confession spree, in the mid-1980s, the media portrayed him as the worst serial killer in United States history.[59]

During his trial, Lucas reveled in divulging grisly details of the victim's murder. The jury, repulsed by what they heard, quickly returned a guilty verdict. However, Lucas complicated matters by later claiming he had lied to the police about this murder and many others because he loved to receive publicity. Reporters discovered evidence that he may have been working at a roofing job in Florida on the day of the woman's death.

During his trial, Henry Lee Lucas shocked the jury by revealing grisly details of the victim's murder.

A Warning from Prison

George W. Bush's steps to reform Texas's juvenile justice system garnered praise from supporters and rebuke from opponents. An individual directly affected by the changes, a sixteen-year-old inmate in a
detention center, wrote a November 1995 cautionary letter to his
younger brother, parts of which were reprinted in the *Washington
Post:*

> Rules are changin bud-dy! They're shavin heads, puttin us in or-
> ange coveralls that say "county jail" across the back. And
> they're marching us military style and makeing us drop and do
> 50 [pushups] for talking in line, or even worse, for looking out
> the corner of your eye instead of looking straight ahead. Ain't
> no joke.

The information clearly cast doubt on Lucas's guilt, even
though prosecutors still believed he killed the woman. Lucas
seemed to know details of the crime that only the murderer
would know, such as the exact location where the body had
been placed. Outraged individuals argued that even if he had
not murdered this victim, Lucas certainly had committed other
crimes for which he deserved death. The manner in which Lucas
divulged details about his crimes sickened observers and made
it easy to favor his execution.

In June 1998 Bush concluded that since Lucas's guilt was in
doubt, he had to change the sentence from death to life in prison
without any chance of parole. Though Bush's action initially en-
raged voters, he did not lose significant support once the emotional reaction subsided.

The 1998 Gubernatorial Campaign

Amid the publicity of the Tucker and Lucas cases, Bush embarked
on his second race for governor. Since some of his supporters had
raised the possibility of an eventual Bush run at the presidency,
this election carried more import than usual. A solid showing
could boost Bush's chances in the Republican Party, while a poor
outcome would most likely remove him from contention.

In the campaign against Democratic candidate Garry
Mauro, Bush took steps to broaden his appeal among Hispanics,
females, and younger voters. He aired Spanish-language ads and

*Texas gubernatorial candidate Garry Mauro and President Bill Clinton
wave to a crowd during a 1998 fundraiser.*

stressed that every child in the state, whether from a rich or poor
family, should receive a quality education.

At each opportunity, Bush referred to himself as a "compassionate conservative," an individual who opposed massive government involvement in social programs out of concern for
individuals. He claimed that he cared about people and that reliance on government aid destroyed an individual's sense of responsibility.

In the November election, Bush won by an overwhelming
67 percent to 33 percent margin and captured almost half the
Hispanic vote, something not even his father had accomplished.
Bush's popularity was reflected throughout the state—every
Republican running for statewide office won.

The fantastic showing at the polls made Bush the only governor in Texas history to win successive four-year terms. The
feat also brought national attention to the young politician and
gave him credibility as a presidential candidate. As the year
2000 approached, he set his sights on Washington.

Chapter 7

"Toward a National Campaign"

George W. Bush weighed the decision to run for the presidency very carefully. Though it seemed that he had been destined to follow his father, he also realized the burden a presidential campaign would place on him, his wife Laura, and their twin daughters. He was not sure he wanted to place them under the grueling spotlight of national attention or subject them to the nasty attacks that were sure to follow.

Bush Jumps In

He first started to seriously consider running in the summer of 1997, when national polls indicated he was the favorite among voters for the 2000 Republican nomination. From that moment on, Bush could not attend a banquet, deliver a speech, or step outside his governor's office without being asked by reporters whether he intended to run.

He added fuel to the speculation by participating in the August 23, 1997, Republican Party's Midwestern Leadership Conference held in Indianapolis, Indiana. The party organized the gathering to showcase individuals considered possible contenders for the nomination. The gala affair brought attention to the potential candidates and illustrated the strength of the Republican Party.

Bush did not make the final decision until the inauguration ceremonies following his 1998 reelection as Texas governor. Before Bush delivered his inauguration speech, Pastor Mark Craig spoke to the crowd. With Bush intently listening from the

George W. Bush is sworn into office for his second term as governor of Texas.

grandstand chairs behind him, Craig claimed that the nation hungered for leaders of high moral values who, instead of doing the easy or popular thing, followed their consciences and did the right thing.

Bush later stated that after hearing Craig's words, he no longer had any doubt about running for the presidency:

> Those fifteen or twenty minutes made a difference. As I started my second term as Governor, I was struggling with the decision about whether to seek the Presidency, worried about what that decision would mean for my family and my own life. And Pastor Mark Craig had prodded me out of my comfortable life as Governor of Texas and toward a national campaign.[60]

Bush already had a team in place to guide a presidential run. His three main advisers—Karl Rove, Joseph Allbaugh, and Karen Hughes—had been with him since 1994 and had earned the nickname "The Iron Triangle" among politicians and reporters because they so totally controlled Bush's schedule, speeches, and strategy. Because the three had little political experience outside Texas, some members of the Republican Party wondered if they were qualified to hold such crucial responsibilities. Even a few members of the Bush family thought that George W. should select more prominent veteran advisers. Bush, however, refused to replace the trio.

Karl Rove became the campaign's chief strategist. He formulated Bush's stance on issues and helped construct an overall theme for the campaign. Rove believed that the country was weary of the negative campaigning that dominated American politics in the 1980s and 1990s, so he and Bush mounted a positive campaign that included fewer negative personal attacks and more emphasis on issues. Rove brought some experience to the post, for he first met George W. in 1973 while working as an assistant for Bush's father on the Republican National Committee.

Campaign manager Joseph Allbaugh preferred to work in the background and avoid publicity. The shy adviser, well over six feet tall and weighing 275 pounds, often mediated arguments

George W. Bush's campaign strategist, Karl Rove, tried to cut down on negative personal attacks and place more emphasis on issues.

within the team, and he considered his top responsibility to protect Bush from personal attacks. He told one interviewer: "There isn't anything more important than protecting him and the first lady [George W. and Laura Bush]. I'm the heavy, in the literal sense of the word."[61]

Communications director Karen Hughes was closest to Bush. He had confided in her when he was debating whether to enter the presidential race and spent many hours with her wondering what effect campaigning might have on both his and her families.

Bush intended to quickly secure his party's nomination by winning most of the early major state primary elections. Many states hold presidential primary elections, in which state voters indicate their preferences in each major party, and the outcomes influence the Republican and Democratic presidential candidates, selected officially at national conventions. Especially important are the March primaries held in California, Michigan, New York, and other states. Those large states carry significant impact on the final outcome and outweigh those of smaller states, like New Hampshire or Iowa. Even if Bush did not win the required number of votes in the March elections, Texas and Florida—his state and the state governed by his brother Jeb— held their primaries soon afterward. Bush was confident he could capture both of these extremely important states.

Compassionate Conservative

One of Bush's major efforts is to describe himself as a "compassionate conservative." Historically, conservative politicians have supported a strong national defense, less reliance on government social programs for assistance, and a foundation built on sound moral values. However, many conservatives came across to voters as uncaring because they advocate the dismantling of welfare programs established to help those in need.

Bush planned to maintain a grip on the conservative faction by espousing their views, while simultaneously drawing support from more moderate individuals who favor some government intervention. To accomplish this awkward feat, Bush promoted conservative views without using the harsh words that usually accompany a conservative justification. For instance, he supported issuing school vouchers—granting citizens the right to select which schools their children attend. While conservatives hailed this move, Bush stepped away from the typical conservative explanation—that it handed more power to people and less to government—by claiming he favored vouchers out of compassion for schoolchildren. As he told voters in Texas, "We must not trap students in low-performing schools."[62]

Bush also claimed that a nation led by a compassionate conservative could once again return to the values that he believes made the nation strong—accepting individual responsibility, avoiding drugs and violence, and completing school. While these values fit perfectly with the conservative viewpoint, he depicts them as a personal choice that would lead to a better life for everyone.

Other presidential candidates quickly assailed Bush as trying to be all things to all people. Instead of taking a firm position, critics charged, Bush wavered from moderate camp to conservative camp, hoping to lure voters from both. They want Bush to be seen for what they think he is, a moderate instead of a conservative.

Bush jumped to an early Republican lead, in part because his name drew great attention. Reporters from England, Japan, and New Zealand joined the typical collection of Washington, D.C., and New York television and newspaper reporters who covered the primaries.

In this race, Bush was more willing to use his family name than he had been in previous political campaigns. Since the 1980s, when he stopped drinking and turned to religion, Bush had appeared to gain self-confidence. His success in his first term as Texas governor solidified that feeling. He previously had refrained from mentioning the Bush family, especially his father, but in this election he referred to his connections in most speeches.

When reporters asked him why he thought he commanded such a huge early lead in polls, he replied with a touch of humor, "I don't know. It mystifies me. Maybe it's because I have such a famous mother."[63] He frequently declared that wife Laura would make a great first lady and joked that the same thing that happened to his father—a political career culminating in the White House—seemed to be happening to him.

Emphasis on Reading

While the issue of ensuring that every child can read by third grade is a cornerstone of Bush's presidential campaign, he gives much credit to his wife, Laura. The former librarian has long considered reading crucial to a person's intellectual development.

On August 12, 1996, she delivered a speech to the Republican National Convention in San Diego, California, in which she explained the importance of reading. As quoted in *Texas Monthly* magazine, Laura Bush said, "Reading is to the mind what food is to the body. And in Texas, nothing will take higher priority."

Sitting onstage as cochairman of the convention, her husband beamed with pride. One of Bush's aides later said his was "a face filled with awe" at his wife's speech.

George W. and Laura Bush emphasized the importance of reading during their visit to Royall Elementary School in Florence, South Carolina.

The early lead made it even easier for Bush to charm audiences. When he entered a room, he made eye contact with every person, if possible, and walked up to introduce himself to them before they approached him. One reporter who followed Bush around wrote, "I never once saw his eyes stray from a voter to survey the room. Bush is a toucher: He doesn't shake a hand so much as grab it; he leans in close, clutches an arm, pats a shoulder, gives a hug. 'Hey, buddy,' he'll say, or ''Preciate you takin' the time.'"[64]

The Early Campaign

More than anything else, Bush received a major boost in voters' eyes when he easily captured his second race for Texas governor. His overwhelming victory catapulted him to prominence and gave him a commanding lead heading into the primary elections. One *Fortune* magazine poll indicated that 86 percent of corporate executives favored Bush for president, and another in *USA Today* showed that Bush would handily defeat possible Democratic candidate Al Gore.

His campaign had its share of problems. Bush performed poorly in a handful of debates, appearing uncertain in answering unexpected questions. During an interview on the cable television network C-SPAN, he constantly swayed his head and seemed uninterested in part of the broadcast.

Since he was now spending more time in the national arena, Bush suffered setbacks in Texas, where he no longer found the

Democratic presidential candidate Al Gore.

time to personally meet with legislators. Thus some of his proposals stalled in legislative committees, in part because lawmak-
ers were displeased that Bush was busy campaigning. The joke
around the Texas House of Representatives was that anyone
could get into Bush's office to see him—if they were from a state
hosting a presidential primary.

Bush's inexperience in national politics also posed problems. Though polished on state issues, in a presidential campaign he had to broaden the appeal of issues to grab the interest
of voters across the nation. As he did in Texas, he made education a centerpiece of his campaign by declaring that while the
government should not regulate every aspect of education, it
had a responsibility to ensure that every child could read by the
third grade.

When he spoke of welfare reform, Bush turned to one of his
father's old platforms—the use of volunteers and civic organizations to replace massive government programs. George W. labeled these "faith-based groups" because many are offered by
local churches. He contended that such groups enjoyed success
with reforming drug addicts, helping single mothers leave the
public assistance rolls, and restoring dignity to human beings,
and stated that they could do even more on a national scale.

Bush repeatedly emphasized that he would restore honesty
and decency to Washington. Voters appeared disgusted with recent political scandals, especially President Bill Clinton's affair
with a White House aide and his subsequent attempt to cover it
up. Bush promised a new atmosphere of trust and old-fashioned
values.

Drugs and Vietnam

Two matters from the past returned to haunt Bush—his entry
into the National Guard during the Vietnam War and rumors of
drug use in the 1970s. Bush countered charges that he entered
the Texas Air National Guard to evade the draft and Vietnam by
again claiming that he simply wanted to be a pilot. He reminded
challengers that he did nothing illegal and that many others had
selected the National Guard as their method of service.

Bush faced a larger problem dismissing concerns over his possible past drug use. Reporters hounded him or his aides for an answer about whether he had used drugs, to which the Bush camp replied that a matter from thirty years ago was no longer relevant. Bush found it amazing that rumors could so dominate a campaign. He refused to give in to what was, in his view, the tactic of trying to destroy a candidate with ugly and irrelevant gossip.

Of reporters who kept the issue alive, Bush writes, "They worship at the altar of public confession, demanding that candidates tell all. They want to conduct a public strip search, throwing out a question here and a rumor there, hoping it will bare another layer."[65] Consequently, he asserts, many good people choose not to run for public office to avoid the inevitable crush of tantalizing questions and intrusive scrutiny of personal lives.

Bush stated that only his current actions mattered, not those of a generation ago. "I made mistakes," he says of his earlier years. "I've asked people to not let the rumors get in the way of the facts. I've told people I've learned from my mistakes—and

George W. Bush believes that the media should concentrate on his current actions instead of the mistakes he made in the past.

I have. And I'm going to leave it at that. What I did 20 to 30 years ago, in my judgment, is irrelevant."[66] Besides, he contended, marriage changed him. He may have been young and irresponsible years ago, but he matured once he married Laura and had the twins.

Bush survived a November 1999 incident when an unauthorized biography by J. H. Hatfield, *Fortunate Son*, briefly appeared on bookshelves. The book could have inflicted irreparable harm to Bush's reputation because Hatfield claimed to offer evidence that the presidential hopeful had been arrested in 1972 for possession of cocaine. Hatfield added that the matter had been quietly dropped due to pressure applied by Bush's father.

However, the *Dallas Morning News* revealed that Hatfield was a convicted felon who had been imprisoned for trying to arrange the murder of a coworker. Investigators checked the supposed details of Hatfield's book only to find that the book contained factual errors, that Hatfield's sources were anonymous, and that he had no evidence to back up his statements. In light of the overwhelming information against Hatfield, his publisher recalled all seventy thousand copies of the book in circulation and destroyed them, along with twenty thousand others stored in a warehouse.

To the Primaries

As the 2000 presidential election headed into the winter and spring primaries, Bush remained the frontrunner to capture the Republican nomination. However, repeated attacks from opponents cut into his margin. The religious right, a conservative Christian coalition, charged that Bush had abandoned the moral principles it favored in his attempt to capture support from moderate voters. Environmentalists claimed that Texas contained the worst smog in the nation and that Bush was more concerned with giving advantages to businesses than he was with protecting the environment.

Neil Carman, a director for the Texas Sierra Club, an environmentalist group, notes, "People are saying [of Bush], 'Is he green George [pro-environmental] or toxic George [anti-environmental]?' I say he's toxic George. Texas is a mess."[67]

While environmentalists castigate Bush for allowing Texas cities to suffer 71 of the nation's 107 smoggiest days in 1999, Bush spokesman Scott McClellan responded that under Bush, Texas smog had been reduced by more than 40 percent.

Critics assailed Bush's contention that he cared about people by pointing to his veto in Texas of a plan to reduce the power of managed-care health organizations. He had a chance, they claimed, to eliminate abuses such as the giant corporations' refusal to pay for emergency-room care, denial of experimental health programs, and their questioning of expensive courses of treatment. The critics stated if Bush were truly concerned for people, as he asserted by describing himself as a compassionate conservative, he would have favored the legislation.

Other opponents argued that Bush possessed a below-average intellect that precluded his grasping the core of issues. Bush answered that he did not need to be expert in every area because he relied on his advisers: "It's just a matter of judgment. It's a matter of a person in my position sorting out, amongst all the voices, who's got the best judgment, who's got the best common sense."[68]

Bush enjoyed a commanding lead early in 2000, although his margin dwindled from the previous year. In Michigan, for instance, in three months his edge over rival Republican candidate John McCain dropped forty percentage points. Voters in New Hampshire, a state once thought safely in the Bush column, handed McCain a surprise victory in its February primary.

Republican presidential candidate John McCain defeated George W. Bush in the February 2000 New Hampshire primary.

Bush regained momentum one week after New Hampshire by handily winning South Carolina's primary. On February 22, however, Michigan voters turned out in record numbers to deliver a resounding triumph to John McCain. The loss was especially bitter to Bush since every top Republican leader in Michigan, including the state's governor, had actively promoted him.

After the New Hampshire and Michigan defeats, Bush reneged on his promise to run a positive campaign. He attacked McCain as being an insider, who had worked only in Washington, D.C., and who was dominated by career politicians. Bush cast himself as the outsider who would enter office, eliminate the entrenched power of established political groups, and restore the voice and influence of the common voter. In that manner, he hoped to enter the White House as president, just as his father had done twelve years earlier. This feat had not been accomplished since 1825, when John Quincy Adams took the oath of office as the country's sixth chief executive, twenty-eight years after his father, John Adams, was sworn in.

Notes

Introduction: Politics Was in His Blood

1. Quoted in Bill Minutaglio, *First Son: George W. Bush and the Bush Family Dynasty.* New York: Random House, 1999, p. 300.
2. Quoted in Minutaglio, *First Son,* p. 277.

Chapter 1: "He Was Always Such Fun"

3. Quoted in Pamela Colloff, "The Son Rises," *Texas Monthly,* June 1999, p. 3.
4. George W. Bush, *A Charge to Keep.* New York: William Morrow, 1999, p. 16.
5. Quoted in George Lardner Jr. and Lois Romano, "Tragedy Created Bush Mother-Son Bond," *Washington Post,* July 26, 1999, p. 10.
6. Quoted in Lardner and Romano, "Tragedy Created Bush Mother-Son Bond," p. 11.
7. Barbara Bush, *Barbara Bush: A Memoir.* New York: St. Martin's, 1994, p. 43.
8. Quoted in Lardner and Romano, "Tragedy Created Bush Mother-Son Bond," p. 8.
9. Barbara Bush, *Barbara Bush,* p. 50.
10. Quoted in Lardner and Romano, "Tragedy Created Bush Mother-Son Bond," p. 6.

Chapter 2: "He Liked Being Liked"

11. Quoted in Helen Thorpe, "Go East, Young Man," *Texas Monthly,* June 1999, p. 1.
12. Barbara Bush, *Barbara Bush,* p. 60.

13. Quoted in Minutaglio, *First Son,* p. 73.
14. Quoted in Minutaglio, *First Son,* p. 69.
15. Quoted in Lois Romano and George Lardner Jr., "So-So Student but a Campus Mover," *Washington Post,* July 27, 1999, pp. 4–5.
16. Quoted in Romano and Lardner, "So-So Student but a Campus Mover," p. 9.
17. Quoted in Lois Romano and George Lardner Jr., "Bush's Life-Changing Year," *Washington Post,* July 25, 1999, p. 2.
18. Quoted in Minutaglio, *First Son,* p. 86.
19. Quoted in Minutaglio, *First Son,* p. 112.
20. Quoted in Minutaglio, *First Son,* p. 85.
21. Quoted in Minutaglio, *First Son,* p. 90.

Chapter 3: "A Much More Intelligent Approach"

22. Quoted in Skip Hollandsworth, "Younger, Wilder?" *Texas Monthly,* June 1999, p. 3.
23. Quoted in George Lardner Jr. and Lois Romano, "At Height of Vietnam, Bush Picks Guard," *Washington Post,* July 28, 1999, p. 6.
24. Quoted in Lardner and Romano, "At Height of Vietnam, Bush Picks Guard," p. 3.
25. Quoted in Minutaglio, *First Son,* p. 126.
26. Quoted in Lardner and Romano, "At Height of Vietnam, Bush Picks Guard," p. 9.
27. Quoted in Hollandsworth, "Younger, Wilder?" p. 3.
28. George W. Bush, *A Charge to Keep,* p. 58.
29. Quoted in Minutaglio, *First Son,* pp. 155–56.
30. Quoted in Minutaglio, *First Son,* p. 164.

Chapter 4: "To Have People Excited"

31. Quoted in Minutaglio, *First Son,* p. 176.
32. George W. Bush, *A Charge to Keep,* p. 79.
33. Quoted in Minutaglio, *First Son,* p. 184.
34. Quoted in Minutaglio, *First Son,* p. 185.
35. Quoted in Lois Romano and George Lardner Jr., "Young Bush, a Political Natural, Revs Up," *Washington Post,* July 29, 1999, pp. 2–3.

36. Quoted in Romano and Lardner, "Young Bush, a Political Natural, Revs Up," p. 8.

37 Quoted in Romano and Lardner, "Young Bush, a Political Natural, Revs Up," p. 8.

38. Quoted in Patricia Kilday Hart, "Not So Great in '78," *Texas Monthly,* June 1999, p. 5.

39. Quoted in Hart, "Not So Great in '78," p. 1.

40. Quoted in Romano and Lardner, "Young Bush, a Political Natural, Revs Up," p. 11.

Chapter 5: "You Need To Do Something on Your Own"

41. Quoted in George Lardner Jr. and Lois Romano, "Bush Name Helps Fuel Oil Dealings," *Washington Post,* July 30, 1999, p. 9.

42. Quoted in Lardner and Romano, "Bush Name Helps Fuel Oil Dealings," p. 1.

43. George W. Bush, *A Charge to Keep,* p. 136.

44. Quoted in Romano and Lardner, "Bush's Life-Changing Year," p. 8.

45. Quoted in Romano and Lardner, "Bush's Life-Changing Year," pp. 11–12.

46. Quoted in Evan Smith, "George, Washington: What His First Stint There Taught Him About Loyalty," *Texas Monthly,* June 1999, p. 3.

47. Quoted in Minutaglio, *First Son,* p. 221.

48. Quoted in Lois Romano and George Lardner Jr., "Bush's Move Up to the Majors," *Washington Post,* July 31, 1999, p. 4.

49. Quoted in Romano and Lardner, "Bush's Move Up to the Majors," p. 8.

Chapter 6: "He's a Seller"

50. George W. Bush, *A Charge to Keep,* p. 25.

51. Quoted in Minutaglio, *First Son,* p. 281.

52. Quoted in Romano and Lardner, "Bush's Life-Changing Year," p. 12.

53. Quoted in Minutaglio, *First Son,* p. 282.

54. Quoted in Romano and Lardner, "Bush's Move Up to the Majors," p. 15.

55. Quoted in Paul Burka, "The W. Nobody Knows: What He's Like in Real Life," *Texas Monthly,* June 1999, p. 7.

56. George W. Bush, *A Charge to Keep,* p. 69.

57. Quoted in Paul Burka, "Has Governor Bush Monkeyed Around with Business?" *Texas Monthly,* June 1999, p. 7.

58. George W. Bush, *A Charge to Keep,* pp. 154–55.

59. George W. Bush, *A Charge to Keep,* p. 155.

Chapter 7: "Toward a National Campaign"

60. George W. Bush, *A Charge to Keep,* p. 13.

61. Quoted in Dan Balz, "Team Bush: The Iron Triangle," *Washington Post,* July 23, 1999, p. 7.

62. Quoted in Paul Burka, "Grading George W.," *Texas Monthly,* March 1999, p. 3.

63. Quoted in Paul Burka, "President Bush?" *Texas Monthly,* July 1998, p. 4.

64. Quoted in Burka, "President Bush?" p. 7.

65. George W. Bush, *A Charge to Keep,* p. 134.

66. Quoted in Romano and Lardner, "Bush's Life-Changing Year," p. 13.

67. Quoted in Seth Borenstein, "Environmentalists Hope Texas Smog Will Choke Bush," *Detroit Free Press,* October 19, 1999, p. 7A.

68. Quoted in Walter Shapiro, "Apt Student Bush Making the Grade," *USA Today,* November 12, 1999, p. 12A.

Important Dates in the Life of George W. Bush

1946

George Walker Bush is born in New Haven, Connecticut, on July 6.

1948

The Bush family moves to Odessa, Texas.

1961

Enters Phillips Academy in Andover, Maine.

1964

Works as a campaign aide for his father's Senate race; enters Yale University in September.

1968

Interviews for the Texas Air National Guard on May 27; graduates from Yale on June 10; leaves for one year of flight training at Moody Air Force Base in Georgia.

1973

Enters Harvard Business School in September.

1975

Graduates from Harvard Business School; heads to Midland, Texas, to work in the oil industry.

1977

Meets Laura Welch at a barbecue; organizes his first company, Arbusto; decides to run in the 1978 congressional race in July; marries Laura Welch on November 5.

1978

Wins the primary election in June; loses in the November general election.

1981

Bush's father becomes vice president of the United States; Laura gives birth to twin daughters, Jenna Welch and Barbara Pierce Bush, on November 25.

1985

Discusses religion with the Reverend Billy Graham and finds renewed religious conviction in his personal life.

1988

George Herbert Walker Bush is elected president of the United States in November.

1989

With a group of investors, purchases the Texas Rangers baseball club in April.

1994

Defeats Ann Richards in the Texas gubernatorial race.

1998

Wins a second consecutive term as governor in November.

1999

Enters the presidential race.

For Further Reading

Dawson Bell, "Bush Lead Shrinks in State, but Still Is Big," *Detroit Free Press,* December 17, 1999. The writer summarizes Bush's efforts in Michigan.

Seth Borenstein, "Environmentalists Hope Texas Smog Will Choke Bush," *Detroit Free Press,* October 19, 1999. An illuminating piece detailing considerable criticism of Bush from environmentalists.

Paul Burka, "Grading George W.," *Texas Monthly,* March 1999. This article focuses on the positives and negatives of Bush's early involvement in the presidential campaign.

Paul Burka, "President Bush?" *Texas Monthly,* July 1998. Burka takes a look at Bush's decision to become a presidential candidate.

Gregory Curtis, "Scattered Applause," *Texas Monthly,* March 1997. Curtis examines some of the issues of the 2000 campaign.

Free Press News Service, "Bradley Fights Back, Attacking Gore's Health Plan," *Detroit Free Press,* November 9, 1999. The article summarizes the major presidential candidates, their strengths and weaknesses, and their stance on issues.

Free Press News Service, "McCain Narrows Gap on Bush," *Detroit Free Press,* November 5, 1999. This article discusses Bush's efforts in New Hampshire.

Nat Hentoff, "The Accuracy That's Owed to Readers," *San Diego Union-Tribune,* November 1, 1999. Hentoff, who built an admirable reputation as a book editor, looks at the controversy over J. H. Hatfield's withdrawn biography of Bush.

Jim Puzzanghera, "Bush Not Top Pick of All in GOP," *Detroit Free Press,* October 12, 1999. Examines a few of the groups that oppose Bush's entry into the presidential campaign.

Walter Shapiro, "Apt Student Bush Making the Grade," *USA Today,* November 12, 1999. Shapiro looks at the skill with which Bush warms a crowd during his campaigning

Steven Thomma and Ron Hutcheson, "Bush Confident His Money and Muscle Will Clear His Path," *Detroit Free Press,* December 8, 1999. The reporters examine Bush's strategy of targeting certain presidential primary elections so that he has the nomination wrapped up by March 2000.

Mary Dodson Wade, *George W. Bush: Governor of Texas.* Austin, TX: W. S. Benson, 1999. A smoothly written book intended for junior high school students. It offers a solid introduction into George W. Bush's life.

Works Consulted

Books

Barbara Bush, *Barbara Bush: A Memoir*. New York: St. Martin's, 1994. In typically candid and appealing fashion, Mrs. Bush recounts her life as a crucial member of one of America's most influential political families. She provides insight into George W. Bush's youth and personality.

George Herbert Walker Bush, *All the Best, George Bush: My Life in Letters and Other Writings*. New York: Scribner's, 1999. A fascinating glimpse at the life and career of former president George H. W. Bush. He allows personal and professional letters, diary entries, and memos, tied together with commentary, to bring out the story.

George W. Bush, *A Charge to Keep*. New York: William Morrow, 1999. Bush's autobiography, written in collaboration with Karen Hughes, provides a few clues into his character. However, it is disappointingly thin on details of certain parts of his earlier years, such as his decision to enter the Texas Air National Guard, and it overemphasizes his accomplishments as Texas governor. It thus comes across as a campaign profile for his presidential bid rather than a true autobiography.

Arthur Frederick Ide, *The Father's Son: George W. Bush Jr*. Las Colinas: Sepore Books, 1998. This poorly written book seems more intent on attacking George W. Bush's reputation than on presenting a balanced picture. As a result, the small volume offers little of value. The reader receives a clue in the book's title, where the author incorrectly labels George W. Bush as "Jr."

Bill Minutaglio, *First Son: George W. Bush and the Bush Family Dynasty.* New York: Random House, 1999. One of the first biographies of George W. Bush, and easily the best. The volume contains valuable information on every aspect of Bush's life and highlights the importance of the Bush family on George W. Bush's life and career. This book provides a superb complement to George W. Bush's rather weak autobiography.

Herbert Parmet, *George Bush: The Life of a Lone Star Yankee.* New York: Scribner's, 1997. A fine biography of the former president that offers insight into the family's role in politics and his relationship with his son.

Periodicals

Dan Balz, "Team Bush: The Iron Triangle," *Washington Post,* July 23, 1999. This article highlights the key individuals who form Bush's top advisory team for his run at the presidency.

Karen Brandon, Joseph T. Hallinan, and Bob Kemper, "The Name Made the Man," *Chicago Tribune,* January 2000. A superb summary of George W. Bush's life. The concise article contains numerous quotes sprinkled among thorough explanations of the different stages of Bush's life.

Paul Burka, "Bad Medicine," *Texas Monthly,* August 1995. The author examines Governor Bush's record on health care.

Paul Burka, "Has Governor Bush Monkeyed Around with Business?" *Texas Monthly,* June 1999. Bush's steps to help the Texas economy are presented in this article, including his attempts to reform Texas education and attract industry to the state.

Paul Burka, "Not So Rosy," *Texas Monthly,* May 1999. This article depicts problems George W. Bush faced in Texas because of his presidential aspirations.

Paul Burka, "The W. Nobody Knows: What He's Like in Real Life," *Texas Monthly,* June 1999. Burka delivers a fascinating glimpse of the private side of George W. Bush.

Pamela Colloff, "The Son Rises," *Texas Monthly,* June 1999. The author examines the young Bush's life in Texas.

Patricia Kilday Hart, "Not So Great in '78," *Texas Monthly*, June 1999. The reporter examines Bush's 1978 congressional campaign.

Skip Hollandsworth, "Reading Laura Bush," *Texas Monthly*, November 1996. The article examines Laura Bush's role in educational changes in Texas.

Skip Hollandsworth, "Younger, Wilder?" *Texas Monthly*, June 1999. The article looks at Bush's involvement in Texas oil in the 1970s and his marriage to Laura Welch.

George Lardner Jr., "The Harken-Bahrain Deal: A Baseless Suspicion," *Washington Post*, July 30, 1999. A brief survey of Bush's dealings with Harken Energy.

George Lardner Jr. and Lois Romano, "At Height of Vietnam, Bush Picks Guard," *Washington Post*, July 28, 1999. The authors examine the controversy surrounding Bush's entry into the Texas Air National Guard.

George Lardner Jr. and Lois Romano, "Bush Name Helps Fuel Oil Dealings," *Washington Post*, July 30, 1999. The article investigates Bush's role in the Harken Energy deal.

George Lardner Jr. and Lois Romano, "Tragedy Created Bush Mother-Son Bond," *Washington Post*, July 26, 1999. Covers Bush's early years, particularly the effects on Bush and his mother of the death of Bush's sister, Robin.

Joe Nick Patoski, "Team Player: How He Ran the Texas Rangers and Became, Financially, a Successful Businessman," *Texas Monthly*, June 1999. Details Bush's involvement in purchasing and running the Texas Rangers baseball team, and points out the importance in Bush's future.

Lois Romano and George Lardner Jr., "Bush Earned Profit, Rangers Deal Insiders Say," *Washington Post*, July 31, 1999. A companion piece to the article "Bush's Move Up to the Majors."

Lois Romano and George Lardner Jr., "Bush's Life-Changing Year," *Washington Post*, July 25, 1999. This article focuses on 1986, when Bush stopped drinking and began a crucial self-examination that led him to take politics more seriously.

Lois Romano and George Lardner Jr., "Bush's Move Up to the Majors," *Washington Post*, July 31, 1999. The authors look at

Bush's purchase of the Texas Rangers baseball club and its impact on his political future.

Lois Romano and George Lardner Jr., "So-So Student but a Campus Mover," *Washington Post,* July 27, 1999. A fascinating account of Bush's time at Phillips Academy and at Yale.

Lois Romano and George Lardner Jr., "Young Bush, a Political Natural, Revs Up," *Washington Post,* July 29, 1999. This article covers Bush's marriage and his 1978 congressional campaign.

Evan Smith, "George, Washington: What His First Stint There Taught Him About Loyalty," *Texas Monthly,* June 1999. The author provides an interesting glimpse of Bush's role in his father's 1988 presidential campaign.

Helen Thorpe, "Go East, Young Man," *Texas Monthly,* June 1999. A fascinating glimpse of George W. Bush at Phillips Academy and at Yale.

Internet Resources

The *Washington Post* has posted a seven-part series of articles and interviews with George W. Bush. Together, they provide one of the most illuminating glimpses of the politician's life. The Internet address for the series is: www.washingtonpost.com/ wp-srv/politics/campaigns/wh2000/keystories.htm.

The *Texas Monthly* magazine has posted a series of articles examining Bush's life. Along with the *Washington Post*'s work, they provide a valuable source of information about and insight into George W. Bush. The information can be found on the Internet at www.texasmonthly.com/mag/1999/jun/bush.html.

Individual articles from which material is directly quoted are cited in the Notes section and listed alphabetically in the bibliographies.

Index

Picture Credits

Cover photo: © Paul S. Howell/Liaison Agency
AFP/Corbis, 13, 16, 19, 36, 42, 48
AP Photo/John Duricka, 47
AP Photo/John Gaps III, 85
AP Photo/George Bush Presidential Library, 50
APA/Archive Photos, 53
Archive Photos, 27, 33, 57
Associated Press, 64, 84, 88
Bettmann/Corbis, 55
ClassMates.com Yearbook Archives, 23
Corbis, 20
Department of Defense Still Media Records Center, 68
FPG International, 6, 69, 91
Library of Congress, 32
Wally McNamee/Corbis, 63
National Archives, 37
PhotoDisc, 74
Photo File/Archive Photos, 66
Reuters/Jim Bourg/Archive Photos, 60
Reuters/Win McNamee/Archive Photos, 82
Reuters/Pool/Archive Photos, 77
Reuters/Pete Silva/Archive Photos, 79, 80
Reuters Newmedia Inc/Corbis, 89, 93
Ron Sachs/CNP/Archive Photos, 41
Santi Visalli Inc./Archive Photos, 30
Peter Turnley/Corbis, 8

About the Author

John F. Wukovits is a junior high school teacher and writer from Trenton, Michigan, who specializes in history and biography. Besides biographies of Anne Frank, Jim Carrey, Stephen King, and Martin Luther King Jr. for Lucent, he has written biographies of World War II commander Admiral Clifton Sprague, Barry Sanders, Tim Allen, Jack Nicklaus, Vince Lombardi, and Wyatt Earp. A graduate of the University of Notre Dame, Wukovits is the father of three daughters—Amy, Julie, and Karen.